D1498039

A TREASURY OF EPIGRAMS

Drink to the joy and music of life and let the echo of your laughter rebound from the stars, for tomorrow when death takes over, all will be silent.

A Treasury
of Epigrams

by

Samuel J. Hurwitt

৯৯

Twenty-Two Hundred
Forty-Five Epigrams
*consistent with Modern Think-
ing and Living. Fully indexed
for easy reference.*

৯৯

Humorous
Philosophical
Inspirational
Uplifting

PHILOSOPHICAL LIBRARY New York

THE STATE LIBRARY
65 S. FRONT ST.
COLUMBUS 15, OHIO

SECOND EDITION
Revised, enlarged and indexed
Published 1961 by Philosophical Library Inc.
15 East 40th Street, New York, N. Y.

First edition: Copyright 1952, by Samuel J. Hurwitt. Second edition revised, enlarged and indexed, © Copyright 1961, by Samuel J. Hurwitt. All rights reserved throughout the world under International and Pan-American Copyright Conventions.

No part of this book may be reproduced in any form without permission from the copyright owner, except by a reviewer who may quote brief passages in a review to be printed in a magazine or newspaper or quoted over the air, provided that in every instance the title of the book, the author and publisher are mentioned.

Library of Congress Catalog Card Number: 60-15957

Printed in U.S.A.

Type set at The Polyglot Press, New York

A 8778

Affectionately Dedicated To

MY FAMILY

PREFACE

Standing on the brink of eternal time, hoary with age, I see a turbulent sea stretching far out to the dark and distant horizon of Eternity. Upon it, in helter-skelter fashion floats the wreckage of human experiences.

In the mad race through one's span of time one fails to feel the undertow and understand the purpose for his existence because he is deceived by many mythical beacons that falsely direct him to his destruction like a moth attracted to the flame and consumed by it.

The eternal miracle of life and love and the resulting procreation must of itself bring on the complications which make living what it is. Everything else is insignificant by comparison. For over a half century I have observed life and mentally recorded it.

The epigrams between the covers of this book are original and reflect life in action as I have seen it, boiled down verbally to its essence. Ambition, love and hate in all its phases and degrees of intensity will pass by you kaleidoscopically. In them you will find a sprinkling of humor, philosophy and inspiration. It is my hope that you will find them seasoned to your taste and that you will nibble on them in your leisure, slowly, thoughtfully and with satisfaction.

SAMUEL J. HURWITT

Laguna Beach, California

An epigram is a kernel of truth stripped from within the shell of reality.

PART ONE

1 When you are about to spank your mischievous little guy—hold back for a moment and consider the fact that maybe you are about to spank a future President of the United States.

2 Fear is founded on uncertainty.

3 Silence will not betray your thoughts but the expression on your face will.

4 Some nations are like bullying kids on opposite sides of a high stone wall throwing verbal threats at one another, each afraid to throw the first stone.

5 Haste used to make waste—now it makes profits.

1 Luck is a fool's hand tool that accidentally turns out a masterpiece.

2 If you insist on harping do it on the musical instrument —the tones will be sweeter.

3 An ardent lover makes an ardent slave.

4 A mistake by which one made a huge profit is always considered a brilliant move by the one who made it.

5 No one ever gained weight from rich promises.

6 A competitor can find more things wrong with your article than the user ever will.

7 Every person at some time or another during the course of his life could have measured his good fortune if he could have recognized it as such at the time.

8 A fellow being his brother's keeper is bunk to his brother behind the bars.

9 Every woman in a man's arms becomes beautiful to him when the love light in her eyes lights up her face.

1 As long as you face life, so long will you face problems.

2 Ignorance does not bar a man from climbing the ladder of success. Once he gets up there he can hire intelligent men to do what he can't.

3 Don't apologize to your friend for letting him bleed to death while you stand by with a shirt on your back.

4 If you would build your life with the same caution that you would build a high scaffold you are not likely to overlook anything of importance.

5 As dawn kindles light so too does reason kindle understanding between men and nations.

6 A politician's bug, if it gets out of control, can become as damaging as the boll weevil.

7 You can't impress your friends or neighbors with your goodness by putting a halo around your head because no one sees it but yourself.

1   The man who was born with a gold spoon in his mouth never noticed it.

2   Invariably a weak chinned man is attracted to a strong chinned woman and in no time at all he's wearing a nose ring and thinks it's grand.

3   You became indebted to your country the moment you were born for your share of the national debt and the debt of gratitude for your American citizenship.

4   If you lost your money, console yourself—you might have lost your credit which would have been much worse.

5   Few admit their faults as readily as their virtues.

6   You can't actually punish anyone who is calloused in and out.

7   When the task is done and you are pleased you soon forget the great labor it involved.

8   If all the people on earth had a sweet tooth and the world was a ball of candy, they would still fight for more than they could eat.

1 You can't win life's battles by just sitting down and complaining about them.

2 A joke may be seedy but still good if the seeds sprout shekels.

3 Every real artist in every field of endeavor would pay with all the remaining years of his life for just one masterpiece and consider the price a bargain.

4 Many folks make payments on their debts with promises.

5 When a man serves his conscience well, he also serves his God in a like manner.

6 A mean dog is always friendliest when he's hungriest—he thinks maybe you'll throw him a bone.

7 Regret is the ghost of a mistake once made.

8 You can be a spendthrift with hours, days and years as well as with dollars.

9 The craftsman who knows there is still much to learn is more likely to become the foreman than the one who thinks he knows it all.

1 To put out a blazing fire of fear, douse it with an abundance of hope.

2 Some folks create an illusion and then try to fit their lives into it.

3 Where are the tears that were shed over the one now long dead?

4 You are old when you begin to think about your yesterdays instead of concentrating on the things you are going to do today.

5 To make headway against strong resistance or strong wind you must buck it back.

6 It is impossible for one man to write the specifications for another man's happiness.

7 The preacher who suggested that all members come to church in their raincoats the following Sunday got a new roof on his church.

8 Folks who brag about their ancestors find nothing to brag about themselves.

9 A woman can make a man feel older or younger than his years if she so chooses.

1 We can't all shape the course of our lives but it's reasonable if you are blamed for not having tried.

2 It is a waste of time to speak of brotherly love when one half of the congregation owes money to the other half.

3 An inflexible will is like a steam boiler without a safety valve or a bridge without expansion joints.

4 Man is like alloyed metal. You can't tell what he actually is until he has been thoroughly analyzed.

5 Never thumb your nose at a man on a rock pile.

6 A man attracts more women with a full crop of personality than a full crop of hair.

7 Vulgarity is the froth that boils out of a depraved mind.

8 Speak not evil of your neighbor's daughter, your son might marry her.

9 The tragedy of love lies in the fact that there was not enough love to begin with.

1 An old, worn-out, sway-backed horse will choose the shade of an old weather-beaten, gnarled tree to that of a full-leaved young one.

2 Life is a challenge but it will concede if you meet it halfway.

3 Keep kindling the fire of your ambition until the very heat of it will melt down resistance.

4 An epigram if properly selected and digested can cure many mental ills.

5 In the cycle of living, life is the positive end of the current, death the negative.

6 As light dissipates darkness, so too does faith dissipate doubt.

7 You can make your pride your best friend or your worst enemy depending on what you feed it.

8 All you have to do to lose weight is mix plenty of self-control with everything you eat.

9 Gloom, like weeds in a flower bed, overshadows happiness and chokes it to death.

1 It takes only one misstep for a fellow to break his neck or his parole.

2 Youth and beauty can't be bought with gold but gold can certainly buy a youthful beauty.

3 The very worst thing that can befall you is to become intoxicated with your self-importance.

4 Anger, like oil poured on a fire, will turn a slight misunderstanding into an all-consuming mental conflagration.

5 Many a man has spent his life waiting for Opportunity to come knocking at his front door when as a matter of fact Opportunity preferred the rear door and was not heard when it knocked.

6 Love is the core of life. Without it, life is hollow.

7 Lips are humble servants of the heart.

8 Dream your big dreams until the cows come home, then get busy and milk them.

9 A broken marriage is like a jigsaw puzzle—once broken it isn't easy to put together again.

1 Religion must be an inseparable part of you. If it isn't in your heart and mind, it won't do you any good trying to get it out of a book.

2 Before you pass judgment, first learn what it was that prompted the accused to do what he did or justice might be miscarried.

3 Any man is liable to say things he doesn't mean when he's under the influence of love or liquor.

4 If you weave a web of deceit you will wake up some morning to find yourself enmeshed in it.

5 Too often the wedding ring a man places on his bride's finger in time becomes the nose ring by which she will lead him.

6 A pessimist always mistakes a bed of flowering hope for stinkweeds.

7 If the truth of creation was unfolded before us, it would be so fantastic that it is doubtful if our minds could conceive it.

8 A gift will always influence the mind of the recipient.

1 Witness the angry waves pounding against the resisting shore and you will realize that even the mighty oceans are restricted by boundaries.

2 A downtrodden person is like one in a cataleptic state. He sees, hears and is conscious of what's going on around him but he can't express himself.

3 The pangs of love are no less torturous and demanding than pangs of hunger.

4 It is not a crime to make an error nor is it an error to admit having made it.

5 Backfire a fire and you'll put it out. Backfire on your promise to your landlord and he'll put you out.

6 When the shadow of gloom settles over a person he starts reading the obituary column.

7 Perseverance can build a mountain or tear one down. It can make the seemingly impossible, possible, and can find the spice of life where none was thought to exist.

1 Young folks should cultivate patience with old folks so that when they grow old they'll have patience with young folks.

2 A boy and girl in love measure time not by a timepiece or the rising and setting of the sun but by the time elapsed between one embrace and another.

3 Whatever you create, work at it with feeling and pride as though it is going to be a masterpiece for the whole world to see and admire.

4 It is in the nature of some folks to send up a distress signal at the first sway of the boat.

5 A suspicious person always suspects anyone trying to do him a favor.

6 You can tell those who were born under a lucky star by the twinkle in their eyes.

7 A person will collapse more quickly from the burden on his heart than the burden on his shoulders.

8 Old Father Time might ask for an accounting one of these days, so don't squander the days, months and years he has loaned you.

1 Much that is written might have been better for the world if left unwritten, but every writer, no matter how prosaic his writing might be, gathers unto himself an enthusiastic following, so who is there to judge whether the thing should or should not have been written?

2 You don't appreciate the ice-cold ginger-ale you had last night until you help nurse your friend's hang-over with an ice bag.

3 Death is final. The living should bury their dead, moisten the ground with tears and plant sweet memories on the grave.

4 There can be no modesty between a boy and girl genuinely in love because it is not the law of nature.

5 Every writer should know that while he is writing his book, no less than half a million others are trying to write a better one.

6 Thoughts emanating from the subconscious mind are like little greased pigs that slip away quickly once you fail to hog-tie them.

1 It's a good thing for an idler to get a louse in his hair every now and then—it gives him something to do even if it is only scratching.

2 Every experience is like a link in an anchor chain. Some day you may need it to hold you through a mighty turbulent storm.

3 To have peace of mind one must first make peace with one's self.

4 If you haven't had any luck snagging yourself a man with kisses, try baiting your hook with some charm and lead him on to talk about himself.

5 Time gurgles with joyous rapture as it swallows the days — the months — the years — a moment at a time.

6 It is indeed a heart-rending sight to see a man who no longer has a personality of his own because his wife robbed him of his mind.

7 Love is not love by itself—it's the end result of proving it year after year.

1   If you are looking for friends, buy a yacht. Then if you want to know who your real friends are, sell it.

2   The memory of it should linger long after the smudge of lipstick is wiped off.

3   Fury is anger fomented with the yeast of hate.

4   A bear will hole in only for the worst of the winter months but in-laws too often hole in for life.

5   Whether or not you overstay your welcome depends on what you bring with you besides your suitcases.

6   It is easier to lock your mind against the intrusion of unpleasant thoughts than it is to uproot them once they become established.

7   The heat from temper can sour a sweet personality like heat from the sun can sour milk.

8   A guilty multitude can hang an innocent man and by their number declare themselves legally innocent.

9   To man, a day is just another day but to a dayfly, it is its entire lifetime.

1 If you happen to be one of those who can't sleep at night, check on yourself to see if it isn't because you sleep on the job all day.

2 The thought in that girl's mind staring at you isn't at all what you think—next time fasten your toupe down so it won't slip.

3 Go ahead and gnash your teeth at your creditors until you chip them. They're going to pull them out for the gold anyway.

4 It is more humane to kill with lead shot from a gun than with venom shot from a slanderous tongue.

5 Love may or may not be as important to life as poets and song writers would like us to believe, but one thing is certain, the poor need it more than the rich.

6 Some folks are like the weather—unpredictable.

7 Hope lives eternal in the heart of every credit man.

8 There are many whose dispositions indicate that they are allergic to themselves.

PART TWO

1 You can recover from the loss of health and wealth but from the loss of character never.

2 Some folks are so nearsighted that when they see opportunity on the end of their nose they think it's a drip.

3 Your ear will always catch your name in a babble of voices.

4 If your husband's good looks are giving you cause to worry, fatten him up and you slim down.

5 Some folks instinctively know how to live. Others have to learn by trial and error.

1 Bought friendships are like any shoddy bargains—they are not worth the price you paid for them.

2 You might yearn your heart out for that girl until you meet her fifty years later.

3 Some folks will stumble through life getting out of one rut only to fall into another.

4 Santa was a very jolly old man until someone with a perverted sense of humor sent him a scale and a calorie chart for Christmas.

5 Old folks like old wine sometimes turn sour.

6 There is one man who has more unpaid bills and a heavier burden to carry than you—the mailman.

7 Hate feeds and grows fat on the milk of envy.

8 You can't witness a hanging without your own throat tightening up.

9 Wherever you find equality in marriage you will find compromise after compromise like links in a chain.

1 Like exquisite marble, the good within us serves no purpose as long as it remains hidden.

2 You can't hide your sins under a prayer shawl because your conscience is right there under it.

3 If you don't steal because you fear getting caught, you are both a coward and a thief.

4 Maybe it's your self-importance that makes you look so swelled up.

5 A blemish on your face may not be noticed but a blemish on your character will stand out like a red barn in a meadow.

6 Hate is an adhesive that binds big and little haters into a unified mass so that they can spawn little haters.

7 You can't hide an error behind closed eyelids.

8 If a host is giving a particular person special attention and consideration, you can bet your last penny the guest is a creditor or that his host hopes to make him one.

1 The man who shoos away his minutes will eventually discover that his years have also flown away like unwanted pigeons.

2 Politics could never become cesspools if the public wouldn't provide the places for the cesspools in the first place.

3 You can rebel and curse the circumstances that cast you upon this troubled world, but the largest telescope ever built by man reveals no better one on which to live.

4 The only good thing about a wishbone is the meat on it.

5 A man forgets what his wife paid for her hat the minute another man tells him how stunning his wife looks.

6 Some folks accidentally find the key to heaven while others must forge it with diligent and concentrated effort.

7 Never trust your tongue when your heart is bitter.

8 A good workman always keeps his mind and his tools sharp.

1 If you can't control your tongue, try controlling your thoughts.

2 Gravity holds you close to the earth so you can work it.

3 It takes more courage for a mousey man to sass his wife than it would take him to strangle a bear.

4 You can't satisfy a hungry man's stomach with sympathy.

5 If her kiss doesn't set you on fire, consider her a wet match.

6 Once a bad habit takes you over, the good ones get frightened and take flight.

7 Love is to marriage what a ship's rudder is to a ship. Each is bound to go on the rocks without it.

8 The things that weigh heavily on my mind are not the things I did, but the things I should have done and didn't.

9 If you doubt people's sincerity and they know it, chances are they will be insincere not to disappoint you.

1 What is hate but the drippings from sizzling anger?

2 A gambler always figures his percentage before he places his bet, then why shouldn't you figure out the odds in your little game of life and place your bets where the chance of winning is in your favor?

3 Rhythm is the pulse of life, the ecstasy of love in union, and the rapture in a mother's heart at her infant's first tug at her breast.

4 Stupidity is always something the other fellow is endowed with.

5 A sure way to anger a man is to have his wife tell him that her sister's husband just bought her sister a new mink coat.

6 Your cloak of innocence will never get moth-eaten. Even the moths loathe it.

7 Old men walk with a stoop because they are always looking down hoping they might find some of their lost years.

8 Many a man would rather go to hell than to heaven if he knew his wife was going to be up there.

1 The road to fame and fortune is littered with bleaching skeletons of men and women who traveled this dismal road. It becomes a test of your intestinal stamina whether you make it or not.

2 Take an unbiased inventory of yourself and you may discover you have only a few of the qualifications you thought you had.

3 You don't know much about a man until you owe him money and can't pay it.

4 Never destroy the illusion your husband has about an old girl friend. He might get curious enough to look her up to see if she has changed as much as you say she did.

5 You can't graduate from illusion to reality without getting injured.

6 Down through the ages women have loved trinkets—they still sell themselves for a gold plated wedding ring.

7 Bad temper is heat escaping from the embers of a smouldering frustration.

1 When initiative in a man dies, idleness takes full possession of what is left of him.

2 No one can benefit by your good intentions if you keep them all locked up within yourself.

3 A puppy love affair is always funny to an old dog.

4 It is impossible to have pleasant dreams while hunger is screaming.

5 Some names are better than others only because some banker or credit house says so.

6 No matter how rotten at heart you may be or what the world thinks of you, your dog will always think you're a great guy as long as you feed him.

7 The thing you bought on credit was not an extravagance if you had not intended to pay for it when you bought it—it was grand larceny.

8 Don't boast about the things you are going to do and never do and you will never be embarrassed.

1 Sometimes in the struggle and pressure for survival, your heart like the soles of your feet, become calloused.

2 The Bell of Freedom can be heard only by those who desire to hear it.

3 Doubt and despair take root and sprout where confidence is destroyed.

4 How else can a spring retain its resiliency and withstand shock except by first being tempered? So too must man be tempered before he can weather the storms of life.

5 All things in the universe drift on the rushing tide of eternity.

6 Many folks would rather fight it out than reason it out because it takes less time.

7 Fear, like a malignancy, always grows in a vulnerable spot.

8 A good dinner takes a man off guard. He might say "yes" when he should have said "no."

9 Your lips are informers that tattletales to your heart every time you kiss her.

1　A pessimistic sport fisherman does not exist anywhere on the face of the earth because a real sport fisherman can be nothing but an optimist.

2　Let people know you and like you for what you are, not for what they want you to be.

3　You can always understand the other fellow better if you understand yourself a little.

4　Dead men can't talk but their accomplishments do.

5　If a mirror could reflect the true face of a double-faced person, he would be a stranger to himself.

6　Before you condemn a statesman for his inability to run the government wisely and efficiently, look into a mirror and ask the man you see there how wisely and efficiently he runs his own household. If you will be as considerate, as broadminded and as lenient with the statesman as you were with the man in the mirror I am certain you will discover that your problems and his are basically alike.

1 Never let the glint in a woman's eyes fool you. It could be the reflection of the five carat diamond in your ring.

2 A bee in your bonnet can never be as disturbing as a creditor in your hair.

3 Time dulls most everything—including one's honeymoon.

4 Love has no sense of reasoning. Like the wind it reacts to pressure and like the wind it can be soothing and satisfying or as vehement and destructive.

5 It could be that the buzzing you hear in your head is the sound of emptiness.

6 When men talk shop and women talk about their babies, they are all talking shop.

7 Destiny soon rings the deathknell for any nation that humbles itself to another.

8 If your husband kisses you only in the dark, it's high time you did something with your face.

9 Desire is wanting something until you get it or forget it.

1 All marriages are based on gross misrepresentation if you want to take into consideration all the promises a man makes before she agrees to marry him.

2 Right is might only when there are enough men with guns to back it up.

3 Repetition is the mother to talent.

4 A man whose conscience has already punished him is immune to further punishment.

5 Don't laugh at your brother's incorrect English if he sent you to college to learn it correctly.

6 It is much more gratifying to follow your nose than to have someone lead you by it.

7 Instead of headlining, "Bigger and Better Penitentiaries," let's headline, "Bigger and Better Opportunities," and we will soon be vacating the penitentiaries we already have.

8 Why is it we get so exhausted just thinking of the thing that has to be done that we would rather leave undone?

1 If people are avoiding you, look into the mirror, it may be you forgot to change the expression on your face after your tooth was pulled.

2 A person wouldn't regret his mistakes if it weren't for the price he had to pay for them.

3 An alcoholic can give you a dozen reasons for wanting to get drunk but the real reason is the bottle in his hand.

4 You can always stop a quarrel by forgetting what started it.

5 Why is less thought given to the rules in the game of life than in a game of chess?

6 Undeserving compliments are idle words that make weeds think they are orchids.

7 Some people's lives are like the ocean tide. They come and go and that is all.

8 Life compensates all of us for living. Look around for your pay check and cash it.

9 There are many facts about marriage, but a couple in love know only one.

1 Even if your wealth consists of only a single dime, if you are alert to opportunity you can build that dime into a fortune—others have done it with less.

2 Advancing old age is like an advancing army with the wind coming your way. You can smell it. You can hate it, but you can't do anything about it.

3 A teetotaler might spill tea on his trousers but a drunkard will spill what he has on his mind.

4 Hate is indelible. Once it stains your soul, no bleaching fluid can remove it.

5 A drowning man grasps at a straw—then at a prayer.

6 It behooves your tongue not to repeat what your ears hear without the consent of your conscience.

7 Whenever your enthusiasm begins to bubble you'll always find a pessimist around to douse the fire under it.

8 According to the Bible man was created in the image of God—that is why so many little men believe themselves to be little Gods.

PART THREE

1 Don't brag about being an optimist if you have everything you want.

2 There is bitterness in the loss of a loved one far greater than any registered taste on which the soul must inevitably feed from time to time.

3 Blunders are maggots that eat up the profits in business and good intentions in marriage.

4 The best way to get rid of a heartache is to bury the memory of it under a ton of forgetfulness.

5 Life in a nutshell—born, married, buried.

1. When you are completely satisfied with yourself call the undertaker to come and pick up your body because it has out-lived its usefulness.

2. If you hurry over the pathway of life too fast, you will miss the signposts point-ing to the pleasure spots off the beaten path.

3. A bachelor has a great deal of respect for a married man—his father.

4. The last rose of summer blooming under a blanket of the first snowfall was sum-mer welcoming the winter as it said "Goodbye."

5. A dog will not bite the hand that feeds it if there is enough meat on the bone.

6. When some men discover that the world won't cater to their ego, they buy them-selves yachts and their wives mink coats.

7. A man inspired by a woman expects no other reward for attainment than her ad-miration.

8. The woman always furnishes the reason for the man wanting to marry her.

1 If anyone knows why a fairly well-written manuscript becomes a classic and a better one a good starter for a fire, I wish he'd tell me.

2 Day by day our days fall away like withered leaves from a tree.

3 No microscope is as efficient in discovering flaws as a woman's jealous eye.

4 The tongue and the pen always have been and will be the most dangerous weapons on the face of the earth.

5 A mousey man, like his counterpart, will squeak a little when he's stepped on.

6 Folks living miserable lives always put on a coat of frosting to conceal the misery underneath.

7 There is no thrill like firsts—wife, baby, million dollars.

8 Music has charm and will stir the soul, but the jingle of coins will stir the appetite if you haven't eaten for a day.

9 Some men brag about their wives to cover up the fact that they were fools to have married them.

1   Hypocrisy is one side of a split person-
    ality trying to cover up for the other side.

2   Why poison your mind with protesta-
    tions against ultimate death while you
    still have time to fill the years ahead
    with the joy of living?

3   The popular girl you haven't been able
    to date accepted tonight because all her
    boy friends have seen her latest ensemble.

4   You can't chase Bad Luck away by
    throwing your new shoes at him.

5   Necessity is a heartless devil that drives
    mercilessly, caring for nothing but at-
    tainment.

6   To be cognizant of reality is to be cogni-
    zant of truth in the nude, unashamed and
    unapologetic.

7   Bees can turn nectar into honey but that's
    nothing compared to some folks who
    can turn honey into gall.

8   Manners are your inward thoughts put
    into outward action.

9   A lie is a deadly enemy to truth and
    fears it.

1 Very few women object to a man's covetous glance if he's handsome even though she is madly in love with her husband.

2 Modesty can be an asset or a liability depending on the time and place.

3 A person will choke while eating if the one who is paying for it counts the bites.

4 Money is a means of exchange. It must buy something to be of any value.

5 On the time clock of eternity our entire lives are lived in the flash of a collision of two stars.

6 Errors are steppingstones to perfection.

7 What seems nonsensical to one may be God in disguise to another.

8 Frustration may not kill a man but it can certainly kill his soul.

9 Misfortune like irritating weeds often sprouts years after the seed was spread.

10 A coward will not stand up and fight because his mind knocked him out before his opponent got to him.

1 Condition your mind to failure and it will never disappoint you.

2 As a life belt will keep you afloat in deep water so can faith in yourself and your fellow men keep you from sinking in a world of chaos.

3 An attractive personality conceals a balding pate and furrows that zigzag across the face.

4 Expectation of grief usually brings more tears than the grief itself.

5 Put a crown on a clown and the first thing you know he'll be making clowns out of his subjects.

6 You'd be more contented and physically fit if you fed your stomach less and your heart and soul more.

7 A woman will marry a man because she loves his curly hair and then try to pull them out because he's too tired to take her dancing.

8 Some hunters get a license only after they bagged the game.

9 No weight is as crushing as the weight of despair.

1 It's in the nature of a female—even a cow will notice a handsome bull on the other side of the fence.

2 Some folks wish for rain and then wish it hadn't.

3 If flowers could speak, stinkweeds would be pessimists.

4 Self-centered people have nothing to talk about except themselves.

5 It takes strength of character and courage to face life and fight it, but only courage to end it.

6 A friend that never asks to borrow is a friend that will never give you sorrow.

7 Every living thing that ever walked or crawled upon the face of this earth had disappointments in their lifetime and lived through most of them and so will you.

8 Wind and rain can't dissipate or put out the smoke and fire of anger but calm reasoning can.

9 Hunger can make a man eat maggoty cheese and consider it a rare treat.

1 A sealed bottle of whiskey shuns an empty wallet.

2 Even a lion has been known to turn and run when a man with determination looked him in the eyes at five yards.

3 Never mention the ant as a model of industry because it's a lifelong slave to the queen.

4 Just how far away it is depends on whether or not you are going on foot, barefoot.

5 In the course of a business conversation, a dishonest person invariably tries to impress you with his honesty and integrity.

6 Wit and wisdom are born with a man but it takes many years for them to mature and ripen.

7 Heavy hearts are hearts burdened with too many memories.

8 Base hit—When a frying pan makes its goal.

9 Folks who are sure of their weakness never test their strength.

1   Blunders are the end result of blind spots in one's mental make up.

2   Inspiration is a burst of memory reliving experiences long dormant.

3   There is no more pliable substance on earth than truth. Just how well it holds its shape depends on how it is handled.

4   If politicians think they are wise in the game of politics, they should study the way women play it among themselves and they'll realize they are simple-minded amateurs.

5   Bread alone will satisfy a hungry man until his hunger is appeased, then he'll want something with which to wash it down.

6   Luck!—Don't depend on it. It's an illusive substance that dissolves in front of your eyes and can slip away between your fingers.

7   Old age is the gathering and binding of many years into a single sheaf.

8   A person with an open mind, having an honest evaluation of himself, can never be enslaved by prejudice.

1 What can be worse than locking bumpers with the fellow you haven't been wanting to meet because you owe him money long past due?

2 A person never needs to live in solitude if he has banked pleasant memories.

3 Most girls protest for a little while because they go on the assumption that the wild flower easily plucked is never appreciated as much as the one you have to climb high to reach.

4 A scandalmonger first plants, then feeds and grows fat on the harvest of misery.

5 Never set a bear trap for the fellow stealing your chickens if you are absent-minded.

6 A secret is never safe with a man who talks in his sleep or is in love with two women.

7 Rumor is a seed of thought that the wind carries and plants promiscuously.

8 There is nothing on this green earth that is vulgar until man makes it so.

1　Time steals the years out from under us like a sly fox steals the eggs out from under a brooding hen.

2　Slow payers are always fast buyers.

3　Opportunity is short-lived. Often no longer than it takes to say the word "no."

4　If some folks would put their thoughts into action they would instantly lose their cloak of respectability.

5　Not even a pretty woman can raise a man's blood pressure like a letter from the income tax collector.

6　Weedy thoughts grow by themselves and require no cultivating.

7　A conceited man sees himself as he thinks others see him.

8　Why sleep your life away when you can make it up later? Eternal sleep is forever.

9　Every day is a link in the chain of life.

10　When one man robs another—one loses money, the other loses self-respect.

1 Art is that something which strikes a note on the keyboard of emotion and thrills the soul.

2 If your heart found happiness, don't let your tongue lose it for you.

3 Your emotions can't rule you as long as you control your emotions.

4 The only way we can pay off the national debt is to increase the population so more folks will pay taxes.

5 It matters not how great your name, title or estate is, in a hundred years you will be worth no more than the clay of an unknown in Potter's Field.

6 Some folks feel that anything they do for others is a sacrifice but what others do for them is their due.

7 Enjoy the good things in this world. You will be too old to enjoy them in the next.

8 You can never acquire the object of your dreams until you wake up.

9 What is sorrow but memories that drill the brain like devouring maggots.

1 As darkness dissolves in the flood of light from the rising sun, so worry and trouble dissolve with a word of encouragement from a friend.

2 It is not the years you live, it's what you crowd into them that counts.

3 There is no reward due a brave man for bravery but the same deed performed by a coward should earn the congressional medal.

4 Life is part and parcel of the Great Spirit and no man or group of men has the right to deprive anyone of life no matter what the crime was.

5 Some folks have a knack for snarling their lives like they do their fishing lines.

6 All of humanity are God's children but Americans are his favorite ones considering the automobiles, washing machines and TV sets He has given them.

7 Many a woman drives her husband to the divorce court with her tongue.

1 Why shouldn't the wind howl?—Next time draw your shades.

2 When your associates dub you "Dad," you should start preparing for old age.

3 Most folks never hit the bull's-eye of their ambition because they aim too low.

4 To many folks peace of mind would be as useless as a white elephant. They wouldn't know what to do with it if they had it.

5 Aspiring world conquerors use tombstones for steppingstones trying to reach their goal.

6 Discontentment is a whip driving folks from place to place.

7 A noisy person shoots words with the velocity of a bullet to win an argument.

8 One fault can neutralize many attributes.

9 Spirit serves a better purpose in a horse than in a man's stomach.

10 No one ever wipes his feet on a lion's skin until it's dead.

11 You cannot alter the course of time by resetting your time piece.

PART FOUR

1   Uninterrupted good fortune can take a man off guard and expose him to ruin.

2   If you just love old things don't overlook your dear old grandma.

3   It could be that the man in a hut enjoys what he has in it much more than what the millionaire has in his mansion.

4   In the judgment of a criminal, vice is not a vice until the law catches up with him.

5   Love is as blinding as the flame around which a moth will flutter until it is consumed by it.

1   "Hell hath no fury like a woman scorned," is as old as the hills. Nowadays she's furious only if her breach of promise suit is thrown out of court or her alimony does not come up to her expectation.

2   How can anyone observe an ear of corn or the hatching of a chick and still deny the fact that a Conscious Intelligence planned it that way?

3   A cold wind will color the cheeks and so will a lie.

4   Nature for her own amusement colors the dawning sky in a profusion of red and gold while man below for lack of tolerance colors the earth with blood.

5   A friend's sorrow and grief usually makes one count his own blessings.

6   Let your mind wander amid great dreams of accomplishments, but keep your eyes on the ground to guide your feet.

7   Some folks resent the truth about themselves, not because it is different from what they always knew it to be, but because now someone besides themselves knows it.

1. It's bad manners to tell your hostess you became ill from the dinner she served you and equally bad manners for her to tell you you shouldn't have eaten like a hog.

2. Your candid opinion might be more appreciated if you candy-coated it a little.

3. Why try to get a man's goat if it isn't of any use to you after you get it?

4. From your brain, great ideas can sprout like a towering oak from an acorn.

5. You are likely to burn your tongue more severely with a hot word than a hot potato.

6. Every city has at least two dumps, the city dump and the city jail.

7. Don't make disparaging remarks about your neighbor's gray linen until you make sure it didn't get that way from your incinerator.

8. The wit who once said, "He who hesitates is lost" must have conceived the idea watching women at a bargain counter ten seconds after the store door opened.

1 Youth builds castles that old age will demolish.

2 Prayer without heartfelt emotion is hypocritical, sacrilegious and a mockery.

3 Hook into whatever you are after with might and main and hang on even with your teeth if you must until the thing is yours.

4 There is no master key that can unlock the door to one's happiness.

5 A glance can become a dagger if there is hatred in the eyes.

6 Some folks, as soon as they enter a room, remind you of a threatening thundercloud.

7 Honey is sweet but not when you fall into a vat of it.

8 The devil will always give Deceit a lift on his back if he's going somewhere.

9 Once you get your name on the marriage license, your wife and your children yet unborn have a first and second mortgage on you.

1 To an honest man a debt looks much larger than to a dishonest one.

2 Some folks read the Bible for stimulation and skip the parts they don't like.

3 A person blind to his own mistakes will rant and rave at the mistakes made by others.

4 Every accomplishment was once a challenge to the winner.

5 Disappointment isn't easy to take, neither is castor oil, but if you must take it, take it like a man.

6 If you beat your dog and browbeat your family, the dog won't leave you but your family will.

7 Our thoughts and actions are often our worst enemies.

8 Instinct would drive us to destruction if it weren't for Reason who slams on the brakes at every danger signal.

9 A man can sometimes hang himself by just trying to see how a matrimonial noose would fit around his neck.

1 Oversight is something that went by so fast we missed it as we blinked.

2 A female lion trainer would rather tame a ferocious lion than a broncobusting husband.

3 If you are not popular and wonder why, imagine yourself being entertained as you entertain others.

4 Prejudice thinks with a blank mind, sees with a blind eye and feels with a calloused heart.

5 A simple way to lose weight is to trade jobs with the fellow who is starving to death on what he earns.

6 Some folks never daydream until they run a temperature.

7 To forgive and forget you must heal the wound so that it will leave no scar to remind you.

8 You can never produce a sunny disposition with artificial sunlight.

9 A hen will delay laying her egg if you stand by with a basket waiting for it.

1 Some men, if you praise them for work well done, will love you for it while others will hate you for not raising their salary.

2 One variety of female butterfly finds the male by scent, another variety by dollars.

3 Some folks don't want friends because every one they ever had cost them more than they were worth.

4 Youth does not follow reason. It follows instinct.

5 Big rocks make big splashes.

6 A colorful woman invariably picks herself a drab husband and never stops wondering why.

7 When a big man makes a mistake he charges it to experience. When a little man makes a mistake he looks around to see where he can place the blame.

8 Regardless of race, creed or color, from up high one human looks very much like another.

9 A bright dollar like a bright spinner will attract and catch fish.

1 It's a fact that most men could learn to love a homely heiress with a beautiful bank account.

2 Mistakes are for the wise, not for fools, because fools never learn anything from their mistakes.

3 If you fear you are losing your husband and wonder why, make a record of your conversation with him and then play it back to yourself.

4 There is a bit of poetry in every man's life but he may not sense it because his nose is too close to the grindstone.

5 If every complaint against life would have occupied the space of a single grain of sand since Adam made his first complaint, there would be a million mile depth of it under our feet by now.

6 A man often wastes his youth and then wastes the rest of his life moaning about his lost youth.

7 Love is an odd substance. You can divide it with all of humanity and still find as much in your heart as you had to begin with.

1 Some folks can digest poverty while others get bilious from it.

2 Practicing self-denial is like taking the scent out of flowers, the sweetness out of honey and the spice out of life.

3 Even though you are among millions of people, you can be lost and alone.

4 Intention is an embryonic thought that must be nourished with action to be born.

5 Self-respect is the compensation you receive for respecting the rights of others.

6 In a battle of words no heads get broken but hearts and lives do.

7 If you tickle the water with your toes before you dive in, your sense of touch will always register the water colder than it is.

8 Progress shies away from the mind that is at peace with itself.

9 A brilliant woman should never expect to marry a brilliant man because if he is brilliant he will not want a wife who might outshine him.

1   The man who refuses to loan his tools knows the condition he would return them in if someone loaned him theirs.

2   Some people's tongues are like mixing spoons, they start agitating the moment they dip them into a conversation.

3   Charm is the radiance reflected from a winning personality.

4   Some folks can tear down in a matter of minutes what took someone a lifetime to build.

5   If men could appreciate the attributes of plain women as they appreciate beautiful women, the world would be full of beautiful old maids.

6   The ultimate in bad manners is to invite an overweight guest to dinner and enumerate the calories in each dish.

7   He whose soul is dead fears nothing and no one.

8   Excuses are flimsy walls behind which weaklings hide their errors and follies.

9   You'll never have to alibi for your friends if you don't have the kind of friends for whom you have to alibi.

1 What other people think of you depends entirely on what you make them think.

2 No person can afford idleness without first having earned it.

3 Some women are as cold-bloodedly cruel toward men as they are warm-bloodedly alive to them.

4 The trail to happiness is invisible except to those who sincerely and diligently look for it.

5 You can spur your horse over the winning line but he'll never love you for it even if he does win the race.

6 Some folks think that dollars are like eggs — that if you sit on them they'll hatch.

7 No one can be at peace with himself or the world as long as his creditors are on the warpath.

8 Spirit is the thing that awakens Ambition. Purpose is the Driving Force and Attainment is the goal where you find Satisfaction.

1   A liar sooner or later begins to believe his own lies.

2   Say what you will about a hereafter, you can't console with words a mother whose baby just died in her arms.

3   A beautiful woman becomes a misfit when she finds herself at a gathering of envious females.

4   What is fashion but an invitation to give away your last season's wardrobe to a less fortunate person?

5   There are tricks in every trade but they can't compare to the tricks in a woman's kiss.

6   I've heard women throw insults and I've seen men throw stones. If I had to make a choice, I'd risk the stones.

7   A man can be an atheist only if he believes what his nearsighted eyes see, his unfeeling heart feels and what his dormant mind tells him, which is—nothing.

8   It's a good thing the size and shape of each person's jaw is different or the fellow next door would be asking you to loan him your spare dentures while his were laid up for repairs.

1   Before they were married he swept her off her feet, now she uses the broom on him.

2   The Power of Creation that brought you into being cares not what you do with your time. It leaves the entire matter to your instinct.

3   Some folks carry their pack of troubles around with them all day and then use it for a pillow all night.

4   A man may triumph over his enemies and yet be unable to triumph over himself.

5   Poverty always exaggerates the size and value of a penny.

6   If you endorse a man's note you are liable—liable to wish you hadn't.

7   There are many more crimes committed in mind than in deed.

8   Be faithful to an ideal—never a slave to it.

9   Even though you hold a grudge against your neighbor, help him put out his fire. The sparks from it may burn your house down.

1   The bud of ambition will never develop to maturity without daily sprinkling with sweat from your brow.

2   A henpecked man will always talk loudly to his wife over the phone.

3   Charity should begin at home especially if the wife and kids are starving for a little affection.

4   Drink and the world drinks with you. Go to jail and you go alone.

5   If you must swell with importance you might as well have the pleasure of bursting with pride.

6   There are folks who try to reach high places by inflating their ego.

7   You may be a genius to your mother but the world demands proof before they agree with her.

8   It takes a lifetime to put meaning into the words "I love you."

9   Very often you can learn from your parents what not to do from their mistakes.

PART FIVE

1 A fool is always happiest when he is with fools.

2 It isn't what you'd like to do, could do or will do but what you do that counts.

3 Despair is a blight that momentarily wilts the senses and blinds one to the beacon of hope.

4 A tree will permit moss to grow on it on one side only. Some folks are not so particular.

5 Self-love is a violent love and one possessed by it will never share it with another.

1   There are folks who have a ready answer for everything except their overdrawn checking account.

2   No woman can hypnotize a man beyond visual distance.

3   Many a genius has gone to his grave without recognition because he kept to himself the things he knew or could do.

4   All of us at some time or other fall into a groove and stay there for awhile, but there is no reason for imprisoning ourselves there for life.

5   It takes longer to heal a wound cut with a sharp word than one cut with a knife.

6   Some folks live under the illusion that God brought them into being for no other purpose than to sing His praises.

7   Your life may be as hollow as a drum, but if you are not beyond learning, you can get some mighty lively rhythm out of it.

8   When a peacock wants to display his ego he puffs up and unfurls his tail feathers —a man with a yacht puffs on a dollar cigar and unfurls his sails.

1 You could offer your heart on a platter to an ungrateful person and you wouldn't even get your platter back.

2 Any alibi a man uses to escape a fight for right labels him a coward even though a great president did say, "A man can be too proud to fight."

3 Don't do the things you saw done that ruined friendships and chilled hearts and the world will be yours.

4 You can be generous with promises but promises without fulfillment do not make you generous.

5 You can't salvage a man with a rotten heart any more than you can a rotten egg.

6 Don't blame bad luck for your lack of accomplishment when as a matter of fact it was your own weak backbone.

7 Convince a man he can't be trusted and he'll never disappoint you.

8 Why do it with your left hand when you can do it twice as good and much faster with your right?

1 You can't steal a tool from a fellow work-man unless every ounce of decency in you has been dissipated.

2 Let your will be inflexible, but make no mistake, let your heart rule your will.

3 A patient man never loses patience with the other fellow for his mistakes because he can see himself making similar ones.

4 The future is like a ladder to the stars.

5 In some people's mind God is the exact image of themselves.

6 When tyrants discover they can't rule their subjects with an iron fist they enclose them in an iron curtain.

7 Every accomplishment is another building block for the castle of your dreams.

8 There is really no reason for wasting your sympathy on an idiot. He's much happier than many a tycoon.

9 If every heartache of mankind poured forth a single teardrop, the oceans would fill to overflowing and inundate the highest peak on earth.

1 Shallow-rooted confidence is like a shallow-rooted tree. The first storm will topple it.

2 If you are disillusioned and shaken with grief and can't understand why it had to happen, look up into the starlit sky above you some moonless night and let your thoughts wander freely for a little time. The answer to it all will slowly seep into your consciousness as you observe man's insignificance in the scheme of things. Your tears will diminish and you will be consoled a little and understand much of what you never understood before.

3 No college student should be given his degree until he has learned that as yet he knows very little of anything.

4 It takes great intestinal stamina to absorb the sledge-hammer blow of failure, but whether it kills you or just stuns you momentarily depends on what you are made of.

5 No authority ever made two hearts beat as one by what was said during a marriage ceremony.

1 Idleness is a millstone around the neck of a man with ambition.

2 Marriage late in life is like trying to boil eggs on a fire that's going out.

3 You can never enjoy anything to which your heart and mind are not receptive.

4 Intolerance always keeps its nose to the wind like a bloodthirsty wolf seeking a victim.

5 If a woman can convince a man to think like a woman, he was never a man to begin with.

6 It's a tough break for a fellow when he marries a painted doll to discover that under the paint there is only a block of wood.

7 Pluck the feathers off a blackbird and a bird of paradise and you will see that both look alike—which proves that fine feathers do make fine birds.

8 A patched up marriage is like a patched up inner tube. Any one of the patches might blow under the strain of inflation.

1 If you are going to build a stairway to your dreams, be sure you are awake while building it.

2 Many folks have a mania for keeping everything around them untarnished and clean but overlook it in their dealings.

3 You can wash the mud off your feet with a little soap and water but the mud on your reputation will go with you to your grave.

4 The man who will not lend a helping hand might have had his other hand chewed off by an ungrateful dog.

5 Don't ever waste praise on anyone bursting with self-importance. Whatever you say will be considered an understatement by him.

6 No matter what your problems are or how difficult may be your lot, if you are enough of an optimist you can even find consolation in a wooden leg—just like the fellow who has one and said that he now has one bunion less and only half as many corns and ingrown toenails to bother him.

1 Depth of suffering is not indicated by the amount of blood spilled, tears shed nor by the quantity of flowers placed on the grave.

2 It requires great mental strength to conceal the pain of a jagged word that cut your heart strings.

3 Wake up and stop dreaming about all the things you are going to do with your money someday. Someday is not on the calendar—today is.

4 As a single spark can develop into a conflagration so can a single drop of ink from a poison pen kindle death and destruction.

5 Give the little wife a helping hand just once and the next thing you know you'll be making a habit of it.

6 Adversity is one of the unwanted ingredients in the spice of life.

7 If you are a bachelor and intend to remain one, play safe and admire women as you would jewels in a display window.

1 Don't underestimate the strength of a child. He has been known to bind two people together when the strongest man in the world couldn't have done it.

2 A blessing is sometimes in disguise—so is a subpoena server.

3 Let Death keep its dead but let us who are still living organize to cheat Death wherever and whenever we can.

4 A low beam across the attic rafters has no respect for the dignified gentleman who refuses to bow his head.

5 An asset is something a bank expects as collateral for a loan. Your sincerity in repaying the loan is actually an asset but you can't borrow money on it.

6 It's not the size of one's brain that matters, it's one's insight in discovering what is stored in it that counts.

7 A little man named Progress looked up at a mountain, admired its grandeur and without further thought he cut it down because it stood in his way.

1 A man imprisoned for life counts not the days, months or years.

2 Mature judgment is good judgment if it isn't so mature that it has gathered an odor of decay around it.

3 You can reason with one big creditor but not with many little ones who become an army of torturing Frankensteins.

4 Every man thinks he has some hidden attribute. The first woman discovering it will have acquired herself a husband.

5 Remorse can kindle a fire more intense and consuming than all the fires of hell.

6 Pessimism is the seed from which calamity sprouts.

7 We may be liberal enough to forgive the dentist a mistake but the surgeon—never.

8 Make the most of life while you may for sooner than you think the red autumn leaves will be falling.

9 You can fool your boss into believing what you are worth to him until you make a costly mistake.

1   Determination without caution is a fault.

2   Death is the undertaker's best friend—until he meets him face to face.

3   If you don't ask your friend how business is, he is not likely to ask you for a loan and will still be your friend.

4   You are born with your disposition and nothing can control it except your tongue.

5   Board of Trade—A punchboard.

6   Some folks are like poison ivy. You start itching all over the minute they approach you.

7   You won't die by not getting the things you want, but if you would, you would fight the world to get them.

8   Condemn not your fellow men. Inwardly you may not be any better than they are. What they thought, they did and what you thought, you didn't have the courage to do.

9   Pride is your ego blown up to the point of bursting.

1 You can scour a pig with a mountain of perfumed suds and bedeck him with diamonds, rubies and ribbons and he will still be a pig and prefer to wallow in the mud.

2 Actually a person is fully alive only while he or she is conscious. That's why so many deadheads cross the street against signals.

3 Circumstances could make the same man either the hangman or the man hanging from the gallows.

4 If a fellow could shrink his stomach in proportion to his shrunken dollars, he wouldn't have to worry about inflation.

5 Be grateful for your good feet even though you haven't a good pair of shoes in which to house them.

6 A person could refuse to grow old by dying young.

7 Some words have fangs that rip more viciously than those of a wolf.

8 It is easier to avoid heartache than to cure it.

1 How do you know you have a sweet disposition if you never had cause for getting riled?

2 Sharp words, like sharp stones if thrown promiscuously, are bound to strike some one with damaging results.

3 Your good fortune is worth only what it will weigh in for on your own scale of values.

4 The more a man loves himself the greater his capacity to hate others.

5 Yesterday's kisses are like yesterday's cocktails on which you had become intoxicated.

6 Someone may tell you a thing is absurd when as a matter of fact he means it's inconceivable to his limited intelligence.

7 Today's greatest desire if acquired, might become tomorrow's deadly burden.

8 In a proposal the diamond often outshines the brilliance of the words spoken.

9 Some folks can love only those whom they can dominate.

1   If women concentrated more on catering to their husband's emotions than their stomachs there would be fewer divorces.

2   You'll notice that the man who doesn't leave the waitress a tip always belches as he leaves the table.

3   Your poor relations might be like thorns in your side but treat them gently because you may want them to double up and make room for you during the next depression.

4   God gave Adam strength and a mind of his own and then created a woman to rob him of it.

5   You can fatten a grudge by just thinking about it.

6   A bachelor's caution is no match for a widow's experience.

7   Before you lay out someone's life, be certain that your own has been flawless.

8   The only beauty a lumberman sees in his forest is its board feet.

9   Possession is not nine tenths of the law —it's one hundred per cent as applied to a man from a woman's point of view.

1   The only thing that can change a man's instinct is old age—even then he likes to remember.

2   No matter how dull your existence might seem to you, no one will ever be able to write a story or play as interesting as the thoughts that entertain you.

3   There are folks who collect grudges with the same enthusiasm that others collect antiques.

4   The way a man drives through a mud puddle reveals his true personality.

5   Don't build the foundation of your life with so much precaution that it will occupy all your years.

6   Some men call their wives "Honey" because they know them to be busy bees with stingers.

7   Pettiness is smallness of the mind—as is also the thing.

8   Death used to do all the dirty work alone, but not any more. Now he has thousands of automobile drivers who have allied themselves with him.

1   Some women, like house plants, must be given a lot of loving care or they wilt.

2   Your tongue can make you beautiful even if your face is not.

3   The long arm of the law too often shrinks to insignificance when its fingers feel the touch of gold.

4   Some folks deliberately close their eyes to life and then complain on their death-bed that they never really lived.

5   Sometimes a mistake kicks up an awful fuss before it curls up and dies.

6   The difference between feeble and feeble-minded is in the location of the affliction.

7   A thing is immoral only when the majority of people say it is.

8   Why should you worry about the note at the bank coming due? Your endorsers are worrying for you.

9   Within each of us there sleeps a potential genius that only requires awakening.

10   A man has passed middle age when he feels his second childhood stirring within him.

PART SIX

1 To a man wrinkles are life's battle scars. To a woman they are a calamity.

2 Memory can be a wonderful asset or a deadly liability depending on what is being remembered.

3 In spite of the handicap by its opponent's head start, Reality in almost every race with Theory catches up with it.

4 Narrow-minded people never broaden except around the waist.

5 You can get rid of your shortcomings by magnifying them so you can see them clearly.

1 A man will complain less of a yoke around his neck than a heel in it.

2 Don't scoff at the toothless old hag you see over there if you were adopted. She might have been the belle of the town in her time and you might be her son.

3 When statesmen can't hear the voice of the people it is because the people are whispering.

4 A woman's silence can mean almost anything.

5 April showers are the tears shed over taxes paid in March.

6 Even nestlings discover after a short while that good things don't drop down into their throats by opening their beaks wide and making a lot of noise.

7 Denying all religions, a man might still worship his mother.

8 Desire is a hunger that only achievement can satisfy.

9 Faith is to defeatism what D.D.T. is to a swarm of flies.

1 Even King Solomon didn't have enough of everything he wanted. Up to the last moment of his life he wanted more wives.

2 A hell with fire and brimstone is heaven compared to the consuming flames of a guilty conscience.

3 There is greater charity in the touch of a helping hand and a word of encouragement than in a publicized gift tax deductible.

4 An envious person has a bottomless appetite for the things others possess.

5 If someone is always trying to get your goat, maybe it's because your goat is a nuisance to everyone.

6 Fear is a mental astigmatism which distorts facts.

7 You are more likely to believe a falsehood told by a rich man in his mansion than a poor man living in a hovel.

8 Nothing but fame can quench the thirst for fame.

9 Faith is the foundation upon which friends build friendship and bankers build banks.

1 Capital punishment is a hangover from the dark ages when every crime called for revenge, not for justice.

2 We ought to mummify for posterity so the future generations may see what the specimen looked like who said, "A thinker can't be a laborer any more than a laborer a thinker, therefore, the thinkers should do all the thinking for the laborers and the laborers all the labor for the thinkers."

3 Only an idler has more time on his hands than he knows what to do with.

4 Telling your conscience that you are a heel for having done it and then doing the very same thing again proves conclusively that your conscience is dead.

5 The howling of many voices can drown out a great symphony.

6 Pity the man who marries a girl that remembers all the nasty things her mother told her about men.

7 As the dross is cleansed from the ore so must the spirit of man be cleansed of destructive emotions.

1 Competition can be healthy only so long as the competitors are not sick of each other.

2 You can shake off a fly with a shrug of your shoulder but you can't shake off a debt that way.

3 Catch the public eye while it is open and you can make a million dollars before it blinks and shuts you out of its vision.

4 Some folks waste so much time every day they keep stealing some from every tomorrow.

5 Daydreams are like an architect's preliminary sketches from which the final plans evolve.

6 The berries from the Tree of Loneliness taste bitter no matter how much you douse them with sugar.

7 Suspicion casts its shadow over the husband's head who shortens his good-bye kiss after hiring a new pretty secretary.

8 The devil knows there is no better hiding place than under a preacher's bed.

9 The American plan is to make money and more money.

1 With most of us it isn't the struggle for survival that wears us down, it's the struggle with ourselves.

2 A hen always cackles longer and louder when she lays a double yolk egg.

3 You would be foolishly brave not to duck your head if you saw a brick coming right for it.

4 A man is living in luxury if his family all have shoes and his neighbors none.

5 It is an inescapable fact that nature loves youth and is forever making room for it.

6 If your car stalls and you wonder why, check and see if it isn't overloaded with too many installment payments.

7 Necessity gives a mouse the courage of a lion.

8 A cow never expects more out of life than a meadow of green grass and a puddle of water.

9 The tastiness of your food depends a great deal on the intensity of your hunger.

1 Many folks are like grazing sheep moving unconcernedly from one clump of grass to another without any other thought in mind except to nibble.

2 Money is not the root of all evil like some folks who have none like to believe. The evil is in the lack of it.

3 Some folks so fear the truth that they clunk it on the head with ridiculous arguments every time it raises its head.

4 Appreciation is what creates the incentive for men to do great things. Without this necessary stimulation, the thing done would never have reached even the embryonic stage.

5 Many women try to make their husbands over to be like themselves, thinking that by so doing they remove all of his shortcomings.

6 It's an inborn trait of character for men to make laws by which other men should live.

7 No one should crow about the color of his skin until he can prove his is the color the Power of Creation selected for Adam and Eve.

1 Making money is getting to be like bees making honey. You can make it but somehow you can't manage to keep it.

2 The world is full of dead people walking about because they never learned how to live.

3 A horse when he's overloaded has sense enough to balk but invariably a man in business for himself strains the traces until he drops dead.

4 Some men put huge sparklers on their wives' fingers not to enhance their wives' beauty but to display their own ability as good providers.

5 Common sense may tell you the thing is not attainable, but Courage, if you have it, will speak up and say, "Try anyway."

6 Old folks, set in their ways, are like old creases in old cloth. They will crack if you try to iron them out.

7 Nations confined on this little Earth, are like a menagerie of many species confined in a single cage, all fearing, snarling and hating each other.

1 Pressure at the moment can cause the hand to act before the mind can stop it.

2 Drinking tea out of a saucer became out-moded because so many guests bit pieces out of the saucers every time the hostess said something that displeased them.

3 It's a funny thing that brain of ours, no matter how much we stack into it, there is always room for more.

4 Hungry artists in all fields keep from starving by maintaining a bellyful of art.

5 Some scientists claim that time moves in a circle. A lot of folks move that way too.

6 The only thing wrong with money is that there isn't enough of it to make us all millionaires.

7 All things in the universe obey fixed laws and boundaries but not so with some land hungry nations.

8 Never dive into anything without first checking its depth. The thing you are diving into may not be as placid and deep as it looks.

1 A marriage license only legalizes a privilege—it is not a bill of sale.

2 Search deeply within yourself and you will discover another part of you who until now was a total stranger to you.

3 If you have the right girl in your arms, you won't notice that the music you are dancing to is being played by a cat capering over the keyboard.

4 The man who gives up before the race is run will never know how it might have ended if he had been in it to the finish.

5 A kind word melts gloom like wax in the sun.

6 Old age claims its right to every infant the moment it is born.

7 A nation off key is like an orchestra off key.

8 Hunger feeds the tongue violent words.

9 Even though the odds may seem a million to one against you, if you bet on your own initiative and ability, you have a good chance to win.

1   It's a very, very lonesome cat that strikes up a friendship with a mouse and accepts it as a playmate.

2   To reduce weight quickly, a buxom widow should marry a poor widower with a dozen kids.

3   An obstinate man is so inclined because he knows his weakness and fears probing.

4   Women who have a fondness for antiques call their husbands "Precious" when they get old.

5   A coward always has implicit faith in his feet.

6   Bloodthirsty men find many self-satisfying reasons to justify their crimes.

7   An honest man turns his back to temptation. A dishonest one chases after it.

8   Platonic love is not love at all. It is an infatuation between two people who lack the sense of sexual emotion.

9   A person never tries so hard to save a thing as when it is past saving.

10 The bond of love can be broken by suspicion.

1 Adversity may give you a blow that will shiver your timbers, but the referee will never count you out as long as you are on your feet and keep punching.

2 Every spotted apple is not rotten.

3 A gentle mannered person is more dangerous when aroused than a hothead.

4 It is well for Ambition to be nearsighted so it can't see the hurdles ahead.

5 Society is composed of individuals very much like those in a savage community each striving for a position nearest the feeding bowls.

6 In marriage as in nation dealing with nation, peace demands a toll.

7 Life will never pay off by threatening it.

8 Digging in a cave in the hills I uncovered the ancient remains of a skunk, a man and a coyote lying side by side. I pondered hard and long over the three. After awhile I slowly and sadly covered them up again. On a nearby rock I inscribed, "Brothers of the dust are we, all three, throughout eternity."

1 Faith can blossom only where there are no weeds of doubt to smother it.

2 Ignorance unable to fathom truth creates a fantasy as a substitute.

3 The pebble at your feet might have been the majestic peak of a mighty mountain —once upon a time.

4 Ask God for what you want first if you really believe in Him, then go out and do something about it yourself, believing wholeheartedly that He will light the way.

5 He who extols old age fears it and is trying to bolster his courage to face it.

6 If you get caught in a turbulent river midway between banks and you become frightened and short-winded, concentrate on pleasant things, never on the distance to shore or the depth of the water under you and keep swimming with stubborn confidence.

7 Frustration is like a thief in the night. It robs a man of his manhood and leaves him in the gutter to die.

1   Civilized man looks around, observes creation and marvels at the Intelligence behind it. Show a savage a watch ticking off the seconds, minutes and hours and his thoughts will be identical.

2   Debts always scream loudest when one's pockets are empty.

3   Life is really never all black unless you paint it that way.

4   Love is the ultimate in the scheme of life. To have missed it is to have missed living.

5   Why blame the devil for all your iniquities when you very well know it's your own weakness?

6   A person is never lonesome if he has learned how to live with himself.

7   Contrary to popular belief white light is not a color. It is a mixture of all colors of sunlight in much the same way that all of humanity is a mixture of all races and colors.

8   Not all mummies are in Egypt or museums. Ask any married woman and chances are she'll tell you she's married to one.

PART SEVEN

1 You can't win life's battles by slapping with an open hand.

2 The fellow who is going to marry the girl because her lips tremble every time he kisses her is a boob. It might be only a nervous twitch.

3 A peacock will not strut or hold his head high after his tail feathers have been plucked.

4 You were an awful heel to take credit where credit was not due you because you were afraid the boss might put the other fellow in your place.

1 All of our days, good and bad will eventually merge into the stillness of eternal night and be gone.

2 Of what use is a big heart filled with emptiness?

3 A donkey will always quicken his gait at the sight of the open barn door.

4 Being honest may be his reason for not living in a mansion but it is also the reason he is not in jail.

5 With whomever you share your sorrow and tears you are indebted to share your joy and laughter.

6 It isn't old age creeping up on us that really worries us, it's our lost youth that is galling.

7 Get-rich-quick investments take more people to the poorhouse door than keep them away.

8 Scandalmongering is a crippling disease that spreads from one infectious tongue to another.

9 A man's enemies know him better than his friends.

1   It is better for a man to follow the plow with heavy feet and a light heart than to chase want ads with light feet and a heavy heart.

2   When a man runs out of excuses for his failures he invariably gets around to blaming his wife.

3   If you digressed from all the laws of God and man and the shadow of the noose followed you day and night, your mother would still find something good about you.

4   Some folks pant and sweat at the thought of work waiting to be done and then sit down to rest from the expectant ordeal.

5   If flying termites hover around you, you know they discovered your veneer.

6   Being lonely is like being at the bottom of a dry well. You are not likely to get out of it by yourself.

7   You can't be a success unto yourself because that decision must be established by others.

8   When idealism becomes tainted with fanaticism it becomes as dangerous to human welfare as a plague.

1 When the instincts of youth lap over into middle age, it's a sure sign that that person had a late start in life.

2 A starving man retains the memory of his last meal and devours it mentally over and over again.

3 There are various phases to life. How one sees it and feels it depends on whether or not there is a song in one's heart.

4 A verbal cyclone can extinguish the flame of love.

5 A petrified habit can not be broken without nerve shattering results.

6 A man's mistake can hold him as viciously in its grasp as the jaws of a bear trap.

7 In the December of Life there is no Christmas.

8 Pride, when it is egotistical, is a devil at heart and a stone mason by trade. It builds insurmountable walls between friends and loved ones.

9 People don't live with other people's idiosyncrasies—they suffer with them.

1 Debt is like an octopus. Both can worry you to death once they get a grip on you.

2 The brooding spirit of man's inner self will forever hunger for the answer to the mystery of his origin.

3 The ethics of governments in dealing with each other are always of a lower caliber than the ethics of their people.

4 It is believed that birds in long-distance flight sleep on the wing. This shouldn't be so difficult to understand considering how many folks can sleep on the job.

5 Most women catalog the dresses other women wear at a gathering each hoping she won't be alone in wearing the same one when they meet again.

6 Foul words to sensitive ears are as irritating to the senses as itching powder is to the skin.

7 The less an audience understands what it's all about, the louder they applaud.

8 If you did your best, even though it is no better than someone else's worst, you deserve recognition for having tried.

1   To believe in Fate, one must believe that the entire universe is being sucked up in a maelstrom of fixed forces that are carrying us to a preordained destination.

2   If a man can't be reasoned with, it may be he has no reasoning power.

3   Assuming such an individual exists, it would be humanly impossible to live with a faultless person under the same roof.

4   An easy chair is never easy to the man with a job waiting to be done.

5   Destroy kindly human emotions and you will have destroyed humanity in a single sweep.

6   Philosophy is life in action boiled down to its essence.

7   Surrender your heart and your purse, if you must, but your personality—never.

8   A total eclipse always makes folks think of God, life and death.

9   Let the philanthropist swell with pride while hungry stomachs swell with nourishment.

1 If the whole world was populated with fools except one wise man, he would be a fool in the eyes of all.

2 The same number of words can either make a friend or an enemy.

3 You can flout a man's shortcomings to his face and think yourself above him, but in doing so you display your own shortcomings.

4 The years, like onrushing waves, flash iridescent in the sunlight of our lives and suddenly are gone.

5 You plant the seed of trouble the moment you anticipate it.

6 Revenge, like poisonous toadstools, develops and grows only in tainted places.

7 White lies pave the way for undiluted ones to follow.

8 Tears often well up to put out the fire of a smoldering conscience.

9 Life is beyond price yet many think nothing of wasting it.

10 Borrow and you'll have sorrow come the tomorrow when the note comes due.

1 In adversity, if a man keeps himself on an even keel, recognizes right from wrong and looks the world in the face with a smile, he has indeed proven himself a man.

2 The speed of light is as nothing compared to the speed of best wishes from a friend to a friend.

3 Don't throw mud at the other fellow, the wind might shift and splatter you.

4 Your life is a dead investment if you receive no dividends from it.

5 The base of the ladder to your heaven rests on your heart.

6 It takes a lifetime to acquire wisdom and only five minutes to bury it.

7 Life is a flame that consumes its quota of moments until there are none left to sustain it.

8 There are many people who believe in preserving themselves in alcohol from time to time to keep from going sour.

9 Liberty is the backbone of a nation. Without it, a nation is merely a shapeless mass of crawling flesh.

1   Folks who love to quarrel will quarrel with themselves when no one else is around and their phone is out of order.

2   Some words can sear the heart and mind so they never heal.

3   Deplore your plight for a moment and and shed a tear or two if it will make you feel better but after that moment forget it and start all over again.

4   Why not let unpleasant bygones be bygones and permit them to remain buried with the years that bore them?

5   If you live your life wisely you will forever collect the dividends earned by your contribution to it.

6   A falsehood, even though it has short legs, gets around fast because the devil flies it on his wing.

7   Everyone knows death is around the corner but each one thinks it's around the other fellow's corner.

8   Don't cry your eyes out over the thing you lost. You're going to need your eyes to find it.

1   Consider yourself fortunate if you have only one stinkeroo in your family.

2   Always be cocksure of yourself in every endeavor even if you have to make compromises with yourself later.

3   A man may have the courage to face a lion barehanded while sober and yet dread facing his wife when he's drunk.

4   Some folks dip into the Fountain of Plenty with a sieve instead of a dipper.

5   The difference between economizing and miserliness is in the motive.

6   If you intend to live only on love and kisses, better add some vitamins or you'll soon die of malnutrition and exhaustion.

7   Many folks have retained the instincts of their infancy and kick up an awful fuss when they can't have their "rattle."

8   If you steal a man's watch you'll have it on your conscience, but if you steal his wife you'll have him on your neck.

9   Most women go shopping—not for necessities—for bargains.

1 Americans are slaves, but only to their ideals, and only by choice.

2 The spinster who turned down his proposal in her youth because his kisses were too passionate now has him as a doddering companion.

3 It may not be in fact but it is in theory that when a man borrows money he puts himself and his honor up as collateral, agreeing to work and earn until the debt is paid.

4 Cunning is not always an inborn trait of character. It can develop as a result of pressure, like a callous.

5 Fighting poverty with idleness is like fighting fire with oil.

6 You cannot discount the fact that we are all primarily a reproductive piece of equipment with a job to be done.

7 Brevity should be confined to epigrams where it belongs. In conversation, brevity can become as pointed as a dagger and just as sharp.

1 He who never rebels against Fate is passive to a fault.

2 Before a bird builds its nest under the eaves of a man's house, he observes and scrutinizes him as he comes and goes, deciding carefully whether or not he wants to live under the same roof with him.

3 A wallflower is a flowering female waiting hopefully for a passing drone to notice her.

4 Many a woman would like to poison her husband not realizing that she is—with her cooking.

5 The same Intelligence that created the orchid created the stinkweed. In that Creative Power's judgment one is of no greater importance than the other.

6 There are many folks who hope their souls will not retain the memory of their lives.

7 A man who will steal a Bible is not utterly hopeless.

8 Some folks embalm their conscience before the undertaker gets them.

9 A bad neighbor can't be a good citizen.

1 There is something sad and forlorn about an aging tree that for the most part is leafless and dead at heart.

2 Those who smoke other people's cigarettes invariably discard a long butt.

3 A man in business is not a business man if the business shows no profit.

4 Some things grow better in one soil than another—for instance, prejudice which can grow only in a soil poisoned with hate.

5 No one ever scrutinizes the purity of the dollars that go into building a House of Worship.

6 Adventure is not necessarily confined to hunting lions in Africa, you can find delightful adventure right in your own home if you are in love and she is near you.

7 Anyone giving advice should tread lightly as they would on thin ice.

8 Wishing your friend who is going into business success is one thing, loaning him a few bucks if he needs it puts meaning into your words.

1 Some folks are as empty of fine emotions as a bottomless container is void of substance.

2 If you will tell yourself that you are going to fail, your shadow will always answer back, "You certainly will."

3 A man can be lucky even if he stubs his toe and breaks it — on a large gold nugget.

4 How would anyone know which flavor they like best if they never sampled any?

5 As you think so will you live, but first you must know how to think.

6 Youth is like pigment. Some kinds fade faster than others.

7 Heredity sets our pace but it leaves to each individual his choice of winding up his main spring.

8 There are many things humanity can be thankful for. We might have been born sightless with life everlasting on a planet heated by internal fires depending on squirming grub for sustenance that we would have had to dig up with our fingers out of the mud at our feet.

1   The glowworm without wings is the female species of the firefly, the male having the wings—proof enough that nature meant the females to be stay-at-homes.

2   When the moon climbs over the mountain, climb out of your shell and look for the girl of your dreams.

3   What is the striving of man but to prove to someone that he can do it even though the world says he can't?

4   Life is one long game of chance which in the end every player would gladly stake all of his worldly gains for just one more year.

5   Your life may be your own but society has a mortgage on it.

6   Common sense can get one into trouble, whereas experience can keep one out of it.

7   You can, if you permit it, become a slave to habit, a principle or your wife.

8   A man's mind can always rise above his environment if he so chooses.

1   If you plan on climbing the ladder of success, you'll get there faster if you unburden yourself of the dead weight of illusion.

2   If you don't like your wife's cooking I suggest you give vent to your feelings by going out and breaking store windows. What they will feed you in jail might be more to your liking.

3   The venom of jealousy poisons the heart and blinds reason.

4   Negligence may cause one to lose his money. It may also cause a nation to lose its freedom.

5   A man is never what he thinks he is. He's what his fellow men label him.

6   Many folks seek God, not because they want to find Him and know Him, but to ask a favor of Him.

7   You can arouse some people's fury with one word easier than you can arouse a lion by prodding him with a barb.

8   Diplomacy—a game in which every player is trying to out-bluff every other player.

PART EIGHT

1   A husband will laugh at the funny little
    thing his wife came home with on her
    head until he gets the bill for it.

2   Civilization and the pressure of the times
    molds a man to what he must be—not to
    what he wants to be.

3   Folks could learn a lot from the flower
    that hasn't a scent but makes up for it
    with colorful personality.

4   Fear is a trait instilled in your mind by
    the Creator so that you will take good
    care of yourself without burdening Him
    to always look after you.

1 There is no smile exactly like the smile of a politician pocketing his graft.

2 A bellyful of bread is not enough to compensate a man for his struggle to survive.

3 Some women never buy a mop because they can always use their husband as one.

4 No one can say what is right and what is wrong because it is all based on accepted standards of law, order and custom.

5 If she struck you dumb with her beauty before marriage, the chances are she likes you best that way.

6 A man intoxicated with power is far more disgusting than one intoxicated from liquor.

7 The burden of poverty can bend a man double even though he is lying down.

8 There are numerous types of knots. The marriage knot is the trickiest. Sometimes it holds but too often not.

9 You need never ask a man who saved you from drowning what his creed may be. His action told you.

1   His heart chooses, but because of empty pockets, he loses.

2   There was a time when a dollar could talk but since high prices and high taxes came into being, it lost its voice.

3   No .one would believe that bits of paper could shatter a person's morale until he becomes a would-be writer weighted down with rejection slips.

4   Every superstition imbeds itself in the mind and feeds on it until there is no mind left.

5   History can prove that whenever a beggar suddenly acquired wealth by inheritance or otherwise, he was the least willing contributor to charity.

6   You wouldn't consume food that upsets your digestive system. Then why consume fanatical ideas that will definitely upset your mentality?

7   If you will coddle your credit with honesty and integrity, it will grow strong and tall and will shield you and yours if a squall of misfortune should suddenly spring up.

1 Marriage is a partnership in which the profits are seldom divided equally.

2 Caution blows a mental foghorn when danger lurks, but only those with good sense heed it.

3 The chances are it would take you a hundred years to find a hobo who would trade places with you if you have to work for a living.

4 Popularity grows or wilts in ratio to one's personality.

5 The winner of the race was a winner before the race was run except that neither he nor the world knew it until he reached the goal.

6 A promise to a girl is like a forked road. Take the right and it will lead you to the altar. Take the left and it will lead you to the courthouse for child support.

7 If you sense that the fresh air you are breathing is being contaminated by foul words coming from the mouth of a traitor, close the damper quickly with an uppercut.

1 At a man's mention of love, most women gladly give up their independence in exchange for dependents.

2 Folks who fall from great heights suffer greater injury than those who just stumble and fall into the mud.

3 An earthquake is Mother Earth trembling in her throes of labor pains, trying to give birth to a delayed Civilization.

4 Wealth is like the ocean sand, a strong wind will blow it away or a shifting tide wash it away.

5 If you grab a high voltage wire, you'll find that you can't let go, but if you tell a high voltage girl you love her, you'll find she won't let you go.

6 Applied to national wars or spats with your mate, you didn't win a victory if the price paid was too great.

7 Life is like a novel—beginning, middle, end.

8 Circumstances often lead a man into the cruel jaws of a trap from which he can never hope to extricate himself because his heart is the thing trapped.

1   Absence makes the heart grow fonder and transportation companies richer.

2   In your effort to reach the top you don't dare yield to your short-windedness. Keep going and your second wind will get you there.

3   Every time a fellow's goose lays a golden egg, Uncle is right there Sammy-on-the-spot to weigh it.

4   Some men and nations are like roosters in a barnyard. Each wants all for himself.

5   A man whose wife no longer loves him is like a man in jail with a key to his cell door that he could unlock and leave but won't.

6   You can't race through life on roller skates without taking a nasty fall occasionally.

7   Monsters are not ugly to each other—neither are vile men vile according to their own standards.

8   You'll notice that every time there is a drastic change in dress style for women that there is a sudden epidemic of ulcers in men.

1   Trying to keep up with the Joneses is like trying to keep a sieve filled with water.

2   Death often plays the part of Santa Claus by calling on someone's rich uncle and taking him away.

3   Any man that can be a fool among fools, a child among children and a statesman at a congressional gathering is a proven diplomat.

4   Satisfaction feeds the heart. It also feeds ego.

5   Too often after a case is tried, Justice leaves the courthouse on crutches.

6   Your mind can always carry greater burdens than your feet.

7   You can never awaken ambition while you are asleep.

8   Gold never burdened anyone except the donkey that carried it.

9   To a circus clown, the music from the calliope will always be the most delightful in the world.

10 It's downright uncanny how your girl's girl friends know you're going to get married even before you know it.

1 Don't be too severe in your criticism of an idler. His father probably worked hard so his son could afford the luxury of idleness.

2 As long as a nation is built on a system of stratums, that nation will always be upset by internal rumblings and grumblings.

3 Expectation is like a parched countryside looking up at a rain cloud in the sky.

4 Training will not necessarily establish the course that character will take.

5 Life is not eternal but there is evidence that the spark that kindled it, is.

6 Prehistoric man was as free as the air he breathed until his wives acquired a taste for trinkets.

7 Tolerance is like a beam of light that pierces the darkness and shows the way to good citizenship.

8 A hungry man never notices the design on his plate until his hunger has been appeased.

1   Criticism is like a dose of castor oil that's good for you on occasion but still hard to take.

2   Experience is the sum total of incidents indexed and stored in the archives of memory.

3   A man might escape his creditors but his conscience, never.

4   Some folks concentrate so hard on building for a happy future that they die from exhaustion before they get there.

5   Your face will not turn red when accused if you know you are innocent of the accusation.

6   Life moves so fast nowadays that some folks insist on dying doing eighty or better.

7   The more thorns on the bush, the sweeter the berries and the more difficult to get.

8   What the world needs more of is not destructive nuclear fission bombs but fusion of friendship between men and nations.

9   Did you ever notice how easy it is to find a reason for not doing what is distasteful to you?

1   If a guy can talk your wife into running away with him, let her go without regret because she was never sold on you in the first place.

2   As a matter of courtesy to the world, let the world applaud you before you applaud yourself.

3   If trouble is always chasing you, turn about face and you do the chasing.

4   Every well thought out plan has blind spots in which the germ of failure lurks.

5   You can't win in life's race handicapped by a chip on your shoulder.

6   A distant beacon light on a stormy night is like the light in the eyes of a friend who says, "Go to it, boy, you'll weather the storm. I have the utmost confidence in you."

7   If you would swallow truth with the same gusto that you swallow lies you wouldn't be a scandalmonger.

8   Close your eyes to Life and snub it if you wish but one of these days Life will snub you and leave you cold.

1 Some folks are like canaries. They want to be kept and pay for their keep with a song.

2 If someone is like a thorn in your side, take consolation that it's not in your eye.

3 Pleasant memories are like ripened fruit you are enjoying today from a tree you once planted.

4 Every failure sharpens foresight in proportion to the experience gained.

5 The welcome mat at your door always stimulates a hungry man's appetite.

6 A fickle lover is like a sunset that for a little while lights up the sky in beautiful colors and then fades away.

7 An epigram is like an antique. It's very ordinary until it has acquired the dust of antiquity.

8 Anger is like a cloud gathering a storm that can bring on a devastating squall.

9 After the honeymoon is over, a yawn becomes the subtle reminder that it's time to go to bed.

1   By the way women dress, you can tell they are past mistresses of deceit.

2   It's always a good idea to chop down a tree that's perfect for a hanging in a community where hanging is on the public mind.

3   A period designates the end of a sentence, but for some folks the end of an engagement period is the beginning of a sentence.

4   If you strive and strain, you can make a name.

5   A man is never at ease when his wife sits in at the same poker table.

6   Habit, good or bad, like an acorn, can sprout into something mighty.

7   Even the kindest advice has a way of turning sour.

8   Mistakes made early in life are assets; late in life, calamities.

9   You may have been a gift of God to your mother but the chances are that your wife would be glad to give you back to Him.

10 Daydreams are to life what sugar is to coffee.

1   The little man married to the big woman isn't really a little man if the big woman looks up to him.

2   What are gaily colored feathers for if not to attract and hold a mate?

3   Hard times taught the value of patience to all except those who jumped off the roof.

4   A man can lose his wife by talking too much in his sleep but a woman can lose her husband by talking too much while awake.

5   God is not as someone paints Him for you verbally or otherwise, trying to convince you of His authenticity but as you know Him to be in your own heart.

6   Many a widow has wept at her husband's bier—because he carried so little life insurance.

7   You don't have to account to God for your doings. Your conscience will do that for you if you have one.

8   To a boy and a girl in love, the season or reason is immaterial.

1 A cannibal once told an explorer he couldn't detect any difference in the flavor of a good man or a bad man which proves that both traits are strictly mental.

2 It depends entirely on just what the naked truth reveals whether Truth in the nude is beautiful to look upon or not.

3 There is no basis for your boasting if some ancestor did all the important things for you.

4 Many a man has left a fortune to charity because Death stood by and dictated the will.

5 No person with a healthy mind and functioning conscience can commit a crime.

6 If the lovely young thing became unlovely after you married her, it may be due to the fact she can't afford the cosmetics and beauty treatments she was accustomed to before she married you.

7 Life was donated to us and so cost us nothing, but what a stiff price we pay to maintain it.

8 If you know you're a fool, hold your tongue so the other fellow won't know it.

1   Every generation gives birth to at least one man who comes to the conclusion that he alone was born to save the world.

2   Money has become a burden since a fellow has to keep totin' it around trying to find somebody who'll give you something for it.

3   You can veil your emotions to the world with a frown or a smile but you can't fool your heart.

4   If you can't sell yourself faith in God or mankind, the chances are you haven't any in yourself.

5   From out of the dark interior of Eternity comes a spark of life. It finds a material affinity and is born, lives an infinitesimal span of time, reproduces its like and returns unwillingly from whence it came.

6   You will never get a rebate from Father Time on the hour or day you wasted.

7   There are two sure ways of killing a man—one is to cut his throat, the other to take away his dreams.

8   Life is like a sugar beet. We have to process it to find the sugar.

1 Your conscience judges your behavior and doles out its own form of punishment.

2 A lazy man wishes the thing was done. An energetic man does it.

3 If your wife gets affectionate only on paydays, you know very well that the honeymoon is over.

4 You are more likely to lose your wife by losing your money than by losing your hair.

5 Don't give your friend advice in a business venture when you don't intend to pull him out of bankruptcy if he fails.

6 A man becomes a hobo when he realizes what it takes to keep up with the world and is honest enough with himself to admit he doesn't have what it takes.

7 That dreamy-eyed babe is no babe in the woods but her last husband was.

8 A promise is a camouflaged lie if you make it in bad faith.

9 There would be no divorce if the thrill of the first kiss and embrace could last for a hundred years.

PART NINE

1 Why take it out on the cow when it was your wife you really wanted to kick?

2 Brag not about your insignificant millions, little man. A single galaxy in the heaven above you contains at least ten stars to your every dollar.

3 As dripping water drop by drop will corrode rock, so will words thoughtlessly spoken corrode the heart.

4 The lawn on the other side of your fence might be greener but console yourself if your home is cleaner.

1 It is a common fault of human nature to apologize for the faults of those we love and to exaggerate the faults of those we dislike.

2 When one's heart is dead to emotion, that one is dead without knowing it.

3 As a cloud is charged with electricity, so is man's mind charged with a dynamic force that is forever driving him onward.

4 Few would have the heart to bury a person alive yet many have done it with malicious gossip.

5 When we are no longer young, our youth is like an echo of a forgotten melody rebounding faintly from a distant mountain of years.

6 As a honeysuckle will attract the butterfly, so too will a sweet personality attract admirers.

7 Bad environment is like an octopus. One or more tentacles will hold you forcibly until you cut yourself entirely away from it.

8 Man's intelligence may carry him to the moon yet he will never create a simple seed that will sprout.

1   Just because your husband is weathered and old, don't sell him short—sometimes antiques are worth a lot of money.

2   A woman is like a grab bag. You're never sure of what you're getting until after you have paid for it.

3   Many a sobbing creditor has been mistaken for a bereaved friend of the man being lowered into his grave.

4   Hand in hand, life and tax forms get more complicated with each passing year.

5   When a man is deceitful he is a scoundrel —When a woman who should know better believes him—she is a fool.

6   Too often the word "sport" is used to camouflage downright brutality.

7   You'll notice that some mighty pretty flowers spring up and bloom in decaying refuse at the city dump.

8   What wouldn't we give to relive just one outstanding day of our lives?

9   We can never escape being in debt because we will always owe something to our loved ones.

1 Sentiment is a mental intoxication that magnifies qualities and minimizes faults.

2 Every courtesy of the road is a discourtesy to Death riding unseen at your side.

3 If monkeys had ten per cent the intelligence of human beings and could be taught to speak, slavery would be worldwide.

4 Every day of our lives is numbered. It gives us peace of mind not to know the last number.

5 A pessimist will always predict more rain during a flood and no rain during a drouth.

6 A materialist bases all values on what a thing can be weighed in for in exchange for gold.

7 Every cat would consider it a delightful experience to drown in a tub of cream.

8 It is unsafe to mention the word "caution" to a man who just fell off a ladder.

9 Stretching credit is like stretching a rubber band. It can snap back with a painful sting.

1 Some folks wait for opportunity to come sneaking out of hiding like a cat over a gopher hole.

2 It shows plenty of forethought on the part of a man who won't go out with the boys until his wife gets home—with her pay check.

3 There is no quicker way to lose a husband than to treat him like a dog and walk him for exercise.

4 Unless you are madly in love, no one can convince you that there is a rainbow in the sky after the sun sets.

5 When your faults come out into the open and stare you in the face, you have them worried.

6 Wit is one or more words light as a feather that tickle the senses.

7 A confirmed optimist is one who tasted gall and insisted it wasn't bitter.

8 Some folks exercise their faces by smiling to themselves in the mirror to make up for not having smiled at anyone.

9 Brittle words like brittle glass are dangerous in a storm.

1 If a man in a diving bell could talk to some living creature a thousand feet down and tell him about the wonders of the world above, he would very likely shake his head and say, "It's too fantastic. I don't believe it."

2 Your eyes and face know your intent and reveal it undisguised.

3 If you can't laugh at a good joke, it's because you have an ingrown sense of humor.

4 With every woman out to ensnare a man it's getting so a man needs a female bodyguard to look out for him.

5 Time is perpetual but the time you have to make your life a happy one is not.

6 Sometimes a man's works are like a Mulligan stew. It has to cook and age before it gets the flavor folks like.

7 The little woman that is so frail and seemingly helpless is stronger than you think—with her tongue.

8 Epigrams are bite size hors d'oeuvres of world literature.

1 Bittersweet in life is when you have a comfortable bed with room for one more but can't find the one with whom you want to share it.

2 If you see Temptation hanging around outside your front door, play safe and turn the key on the inside.

3 A man can never get a cut in his alimony if the judge is a woman, and a man-hater to boot.

4 How can a fellow love his neighbor if his neighbor keeps as his own everything he borrows?

5 An overabundance of anything can make a fellow nauseous—even money.

6 What happened to the wonderful world one lived in during courtship?

7 An old man, afraid of the years, treads cautiously like a whipped dog remembering the whip.

8 A man can be lost even though he knows every street and highway for a hundred miles around.

9 Faults are character defects like dry rot in a tree which will destroy it if not corrected in time.

1 A diamond in a subdued light can blind a girl quicker than the brilliance of a summer noonday sun.

2 How can you speak in a universal language and explain the principles of a United World when millions still believe the moon is made of green cheese?

3 Many a man sold himself into captivity for a kiss that was artificially flavored.

4 Your religious belief is a farce if you don't live it.

5 Openhearted generosity is often dressed up to disguise an ulterior motive.

6 Modern civilization isn't all it's cracked up to be to the fellow bent bowlegged from the burden of monthly payments.

7 The man who wouldn't want to die in a rip tide of passion when he's due to die —is already dead.

8 When the world has licked a man and knocked him for a loop, he likes to think he just came to his senses when he refuses to get up and fight it some more.

1 When you pay back a debt of gratitude always add a little interest.

2 Your inability to take life is due to the great respect and appreciation you have for it.

3 If you insist upon worshipping false gods, the golden calf is as good as any.

4 Folks often chase after success in all sorts of out-of-the-way places when as a matter of fact the seeds of it are right under their very feet.

5 A dog that won't fight other dogs to keep his bone never has it for long.

6 To hit the bull's-eye you must first see it, so never shoot at anything in the dark.

7 Give ten boys ten dollars each and sooner or later Uncle will have all the dollars.

8 Folks get married so the kids in the neighborhood won't call their offspring vile names—but they do anyway.

9 Cowards shrink from fear while brave men blind themselves to it.

10 A man who speaks his mind, without restraint soon empties it.

1 When a person is buried his friends should bury his faults with him.

2 How crazy can one be? That depends on who is judging who?

3 Sometimes a fellow's intentions are good but his presentation of them sadly misunderstood.

4 The less a man can afford a dollar cigar, the more pleasure he will derive from it.

5 Make a name for yourself and the world will applaud and laugh at every joke you tell even though they don't understand what it's all about.

6 You can't blueprint your life because you don't know what is ahead of you.

7 Some folks dangle on an imaginary precipice all their lives screaming for help when as a matter of fact there is solid substance directly beneath them.

8 Obedience is the end result of a whip in the hand of a master, regardless of whether the whip is mental or physical.

9 When one lives by himself it is because by his very nature he can't live with others.

1 What any man is capable of doing today, good or bad, you may be capable of doing tomorrow under like circumstances.

2 Atheists are what they are because they were never introduced to God by His right name.

3 There is always another chance provided the last chance you took left you all in one piece.

4 For all that some folks learn from hearing, one would think that the only thing their ears are good for is to let the wind blow through them so they can air condition the space where their brains should be.

5 When folks fail dismally in the present, they become devout believers in the future.

6 There can't be an iota of satisfaction in hitting the bull's-eye accidentally.

7 Somewhere along life's pathway every man is at one time or another influenced by some woman's love and devotion or her hatred.

1 Books, like meteorites, can shake the very foundation of the earth or just fizzle out.

2 A self-imposed rule without flexibility can become a ruling tyrant.

3 If the only physical difference between all people of the world was that some had white teeth and some black, there would still be class discrimination.

4 A person need not be an acrobat to have stability.

5 Why begrudge the other man his possessions? Take inventory of your own and you may discover you have an abundance of wealth of a sort which he does not possess.

6 Idle days and years like unused tools rust away.

7 If you can't rebuild your life you certainly can brace it a little here and there to prevent it from tumbling down and crushing you.

8 It's the old fogies, jealous of youth, that are so faultfinding with it.

PART TEN

1 You wouldn't deliberately prick a person
—then why needle him?

2 Failure takes over and buries ambition
the moment it stumbles.

3 No matter how deep you bury your past,
if it was rotten, the stench will always
follow you.

4 You might as well feel big and important while you are in the director's chair
because the little wife will take over
when you get home.

5 A knowing bride like an over ripe peach
no longer blushes.

1 Whatever you do will be a thankless job if you make it that.

2 A man's pretty companion tickles his vanity while the mink coat he gave her tickles her pretty neck.

3 Life is a speck of time borrowed from Eternity. Being a loan, we are under obligation to return it clean and untarnished.

4 Words carelessly spoken may take root and grow into horrible monstrosities.

5 Many stumble along Life's pathway because they keep looking so far ahead they never see the ruts at their feet.

6 Some children will not share their candy with you but will gladly share yours.

7 The more highly organized a group of people become the more laws they make and the more penal institutions they build.

8 No! No! No, young ladies. An engagement ring is not the same as a wedding ring.

9 Popularity can live and grow only in the radiance of charm.

1 Anxiety is the trailing shadow of instability.
2 It is more important to train your tongue
   to win friends than arguments.
3 Maybe it's the chip on your shoulder
   that makes dogs bark at you and people
   avoid you.
4 Memory has a devilish way of dragging
   out your guilty conscience every now and
   then just to make it squirm.
5 Go ahead and lose your temper, it was
   never any good to you anyway.   .
6 If you can tell the same untruth time and
   again without variation, you either have
   an excellent memory or you are a natural
   born liar.
7 Flattery is as void of substance as a de-
   flated balloon.
8 Is takes many kind words to make a
   friend, only one to make an enemy.
9 If you feel down on your luck and life
   is dreary, do a little prospecting within
   yourself and you may find a wealth of
   resources you never knew you had.

1 An overwhelming personality is like an octopus that grips and crushes its victim.

2 One man would trade his fortune for what another considers a misfortune.

3 When you come to the conclusion that you have been a heel all your life, you have come to the crossroads of your life and from this moment on you are a man to be trusted and respected.

4 If you will scatter seeds of kindness as you wander along life's pathways, many of them will take root and thrill you when you pass by again.

5 Why waste time figuring out your faults? Just ask anyone who dislikes you.

6 Prune the useless twigs from your mind as you would the trees in your orchard so you will bear only useful thoughts.

7 Jealousy is reason out of control.

8 Sooner or later your big sins will catch up with you while the little ones will belch up.

9 Sweet nectar of success is a sure cure for frustration.

1 Love contains within itself the spark that can ignite an all-consuming hate.

2 Adversity is a reaper with a flail that levels everything flat with the ground and sets up scarecrows to keep Hope away.

3 There are things we had yesterday we don't want today and there are things we want today we won't want tomorrow.

4 Science advances slowly but surely on a rutted road of trial and error.

5 When you see someone stoop shouldered from the weight of a heavy sack on his back, take another look. It might be the reflection of yourself carrying all your troubles in that sack.

6 Chance is like a rudderless raft adrift with wind and tide as the only propelling factor.

7 If it weren't for the fact with hardly an exception that within every man regardless of exterior appearance there lies the potential making of a killer, war could never be fomented by a fanatical leader.

1 The insistent hunger in the heart of man to worship and place implicit faith in a Creative Power leads one to believe that the subconscious mind knows such a Power exists or might be a spiritual part of It.

2 Your shadow, like your intelligence, is never in proportion to your height.

3 Show a meatless bone to a hungry dog and his mouth will water—proving that expectation is greater than realization.

4 Many a man insisted he was shrewd— until a woman got him and proved him otherwise.

5 Some folks' tongues are like whetstones that can sharpen ordinarily harmless words into razor edged weapons.

6 Life, gathering all your good deeds, is like a cloud gathering moisture which will some day display it all before you as a magnificent rainbow.

7 Death builds a coffin at every birth.

8 Once you discover the better side of your associates, they will soon discover the better side of you.

1   Complexities of life fade into nothingness as the plane rises over the roof tops.

2   What difference does it make while eating breakfast this morning whether or not you had dessert for dinner last night?

3   Imagination is the twin brother to Progress.

4   The first thing you should do when you seek happiness is to make sure you have a place in your heart to keep it after you find it.

5   Reality casts a shadow not always like itself. Folks sometimes mistake it for Suspicion.

6   A person whose life has been dull and uninteresting is like a book with all the pages torn out.

7   The strength of faith is in proportion to its depth.

8   The seed pod of admiration produces a variety of seeds which when sown and cultivated sprout friendship, love and hate in all its phases.

1 There is no such thing as shameful craving. Without instinct's demand for passion's fulfillment, the world would be void of life.

2 Before he married her he told her she looked like a picture in a frame. Now he wants to hang her.

3 Plant a stinkweed among orchids and in no time at all the stinkweed will imagine itself an orchid.

4 Strip a man of his exterior mask and you will find the ego that is himself.

5 Like an avalanche rolling down a mountainside, the boulders like our years follow to engulf us.

6 Adaptation is a sort of shaping and processing like a smithy forging iron and tempering it so it can withstand the tension and hard blows that it must bear.

7 Unconsciously we contrast all things large and small by our own size.

8 The power which can raise a man to the highest pinnacle can also lower him into his grave.

9 Let unkind thoughts within you blow away like dead leaves in a windstorm.

1 Faith in yourself will kindle the faith that you want others to have in you.

2 Fret not over the passing of time. Even as you and I the days and the years must die.

3 Food highly over-priced like food highly over-seasoned can spoil one's appetite for more.

4 What is fun and laughter but a sweetener in the monotony of living!

5 Men have built fortunes with a single dollar but given time their heirs will reduce it back to its beginning.

6 If you got nowhere with your present face, cover it with a smile and you will really go places.

7 You cannot pay off an honest debt honestly with stolen money.

8 No matter how often you scald a cat with hot butter, she will keep coming back for more.

9 A craftsman who is on friendly relationship with his tools never quarrels with them.

1 The only good thing about an argument is that those involved wear themselves out and won't argue again for a little while.

2 Show me the man who can think of his boyhood without bringing a lump to his throat and a hunger in his heart and I will show you a man void of human emotion.

3 The sale of axes has dropped off considerably because too many folks have discovered they can mutilate easier with their tongue.

4 Truth when distorted evolves into a part truth and is therefore no longer truth.

5 Life is a spark that momentarily lights up the face on the timepiece of Eternity.

6 If the dust of the earth could speak, millions of voices would rise to tell you that you live only once, so get the most out of life while you can because the sleep of death is eternal.

7 Hope feeds the soul and encourages it to hold on a little longer when the going is tough.

1 It is true that if you help an ungrateful person out of a pickle, you may find yourself pickled in his place.

2 You can serve the most delicious meal in the world and poison it with a single word while serving it.

3 A man might like stewed chicken but a a stewing hen, never.

4 The dog at the entrance gate invariably reflects the personality of the people you will meet at the door.

5 There are many who weigh their good fortune as some weigh their gold and silver.

6 Happiness cannot be scooped up by the handful because it is encased in life's rubble like gold in quartz.

7 Confidence is the adhesive that keeps the world from falling apart when the pressure of disillusionment threatens it.

8 To a pretty girl a young man is like a ripening berry on a bush. She can pick him at any time.

9 A leech will draw blood from the veins while a cutting word will draw it from the heart.

1 The key to the door of success must be forged from concentrated effort and tempered in a tub of sweat.

2 The only difference between common sense and good sense is in its refinement.

3 Never climb so high on the ladder of success that you will lose sight of those who helped you get up there. They are still down there below and might kick the ladder out from under you.

4 What good are the years if we leave them like empty sacks in a harvest field?

5 An empty cup to thirsty lips is as satisfying as a kiss without emotion.

6 A pleasant personality is vitalized with a magnetic power that invariably attracts and holds like a magic spell.

7 Truth begets Confidence and Confidence begets Opportunity on which one can ride slowly but surely to the Golden City of Success.

8 Call me a scoundrel if you like, but how else could I be expected to write true to life epigrams except by delving into the innermost depths of people's hearts and minds?

1 Optimism is a positive eradicator for a blot of disappointment. Use it freely.

2 A sharp tongue is like a sword at white heat. It sears while it cuts.

3 Effort is the driving force by which Ambition reaches its desired goal.

4 Confidence is the by-product of optimism.

5 One thing every man is willing to share with every other man is his intolerance.

6 A dog will sniff a man's leg and by his halo of odor decide whether he wants him as a friend or to chase him away as an enemy.

7 No matter how I try to escape Old Age, the bone picker, I find him chasing after me with a bag of bones on his shoulder and getting closer to me day by day.

8 Closing your eyes to a dangerous truth is like closing your eyes to an oncoming train.

9 An author's works are like the waters in a stream that keeps flowing until the headwaters dry up.

1 An ordinary two cent pencil has the potential to make a man the richest in the world, the happiest or the most miserable.

2 Some folks are so ticklish they laugh before they know whether they're going to get tickled with a feather or hit with a brick.

3 You can gold-plate your conscience and fool the world but you will never be fooled by it.

4 A man's shroud will bring forgiveness quicker than his lips ever could.

5 Some ancient wit once said, "Silence is golden," but that was before the game of politics was invented.

6 Self-respect is the most precious thing in the world and the easiest to lose.

7 Some men travel around the world to satisfy their curiosity. Others just go to bed.

8 Don't laugh too hard and too loud at the other fellow's hysterical laughter until you make certain he isn't laughing at you.

9 Peace is like an olive. Some like it, others don't.

1   Success is a wary old bird that flies high and builds its nest in the most inaccessible places. You have to build a long ladder and climb slowly and cautiously, a rung at a time, to reach it and capture it.

2   There are folks who will gladly mind your business and yet refuse to baby sit for you.

3   Peace of mind can never be found under the same roof with an overambitious person.

4   Only those who have never known the thrill and the fire of love put a stigma on it.

5   A woman can look a man over as she would yardage and feel sure what she could make of him.

6   You can never cover a bad reputation with a new paint job without it bleeding through in some places.

7   Some folks seem to derive great pleasure from the pain of an open wound. Instead of trying to heal it they let it fester.

8   A lie is like a cracked bell. It doesn't ring true.

1 Humanity lives and yet is never fully alive because bits of it keep dying off like the limbs of a tree in a drouth.

2 The ultimate and most satisfying ingredient in the spice of life is love in union.

3 A nation as a whole has no conscience but its people have. That's why the people should do all the thinking for it.

4 Trying to be like someone else is like saponifying oil with water which becomes something entirely different from the original ingredients.

5 Love shackles the heart but the feet are still free to stray.

6 Some folks make it easy for Failure to find them by placing signposts in glaring colors to direct it.

7 Generosity is not generous when it has an ulterior motive prodding it with a pitchfork.

8 Every day adds another link to the chain of life until it becomes so heavy it crushes the carrier with its weight.

9 Many good things come from lowly beginnings, for instance—like mushrooms in a cow pasture.

1 Lack of confidence in others makes you distrust them and lack of confidence in yourself makes you distrust yourself.

2 A twisted mind like a corkscrew can never penetrate a thing straight.

3 Dear old Grandma has at long last learned how to clip the wings of time with cosmetics and what nots and now wins beauty contests in competition with her daughters.

4 The honeymoon is over the moment you begin to wonder why the last kiss failed to thrill you.

5 Dissension is like a tangled fishing line. You can take time and strain your patience to untangle the mess and then forget that it was ever tangled or cut it away hurriedly without further thought.

6 Forgetfulness scatters the seeds from which weeds sprout and flourish over the grave of the forgotten one.

7 Some folks when struck by adversity reel from the shock and are soon themselves again while others break up into bits like a thing made of glass.

1   Wherever you find a spare room you will invariably find relatives.

2   Most women could learn to love any man with a song in his heart if the song was coining enough royalties.

3   Some folks go through life like they go through a revolving door always getting back to the point of beginning.

4   Many a couple returning from their honeymoon close the door to their heaven as soon as they open their front door.

5   Death has great respect for those who defy him.

6   Most folks drive themselves so fast that they must snatch whatever happiness they can while they run.

7   Many an heir buries his grief even before the grave diggers bury the body.

8   If someone would invent a sort of litmus paper to put on the tongue to test its verbal acidity, couples before marriage could know what to expect from each other after marriage.

PART ELEVEN

1 A tree unaccustomed to sudden squalls will break or topple because it never learned how to overcome pressure by bending.

2 You can prick a thief's conscience by praising him for his honesty.

3 There are no advance reservations for prison cells. Any one of us are liable to skid and find ourselves in one.

4 You can find a smelly gas pocket in many homes and business organizations that no amount of perfume can overcome.

1   Give your creative thoughts freedom but not so your instinctive inclinations.

2   It could be that if you let the cat out of the bag when you shouldn't have, it will come back some day to scratch you.

3   Scandal is a hideous thing that buries its victims alive and gloats in their suffering.

4   The sum total of your years will never shelve you without the help of your mind.

5   Don't ask for the truth when you very well know the answer will not please you.

6   Sometimes a man will fondle a kitten not knowing it's a young hellcat.

7   You can even find stinkers in the vegetable kingdom.

8   Every fortune is supported by underpinnings of one sort or another. Whether it stands or falls depends upon the mood of Miss Fortune.

9   Time is perpetually being pulverized by the heavy grinding feet of the years that keep coming and going.

10 Old age is like a Christmas tree with all of its lights burned out and the gifts gone.

1   The Power of Creation can be seen in the burst of every bloom and the miracle of life in the seed that follows.

2   A pessimist could never be persuaded to try on a pair of rose-colored glasses.

3   A woman who marries a man to escape hunger and cold will still be hungry and cold after she marries him.

4   Poverty keeps the stomach empty but avarice keeps it shrunk.

5   Eternity gathers its spent moments and carries them back to their birthplace for burial.

6   No war present or past leaves one more desolate, wretched and forlorn than a war between body and soul.

7   The price of matrimony is the price you are going to pay for her relatives.

8   Vanity is born not in the mind but in the display window.

9   An open road to a careless driver is like cheese in a mouse trap in that death is tempting both, the driver and the mouse.

1 Every time a new law is written a new set of jail keys are forged.

2 Discipline without a realistic reason is tyranny.

3 Justice has teeth which lawyers are trained to draw before they can bite their clients.

4 Every woman with hardly an exception will try to strangle or poison with word or deed every hobby and interest which distracts her husband from herself.

5 Jealousy is a convincing loudmouth that drowns out the voice of reason.

6 Spark my dormant subconsciousness and it will burst forth with an experience long forgotten.

7 A gain might seem to be a profit and set up so on the profit side of your ledger and yet turn out to be a total loss in character in the moral column.

8 Every business has woven through it the sinews and personality of its top executive.

9 Self-pity is a frustration of one's own making.

1   Children will often love a person that adults despise because as children they have not yet developed an insight to deceit.

2   A grudge is a hateful sort of thing because it always conceals the fine points in those it dislikes.

3   Never let your little woman know the magic word by which she could make you obey her every command.

4   Some folks are like dark stormy clouds allowing the sunshine to break through only on rare occasions.

5   It takes years to master the art of cooking so if you are a newlywed flavor your meals with kisses before, during and after and he really won't notice the awfulness of the stuff you are feeding him.

6   Keep a man guessing and the first thing you will know is that you have outguessed yourself.

7   Biologists admit that there is no proportionate difference in the size of a man's or woman's brain but they do say that a woman's tongue muscles are tremendously powerful for their size.

1 Troubles are hideous enough as they are without putting them under a magnifying glass to make them look worse than they are.

2 Sometimes a good intention miscarries and gives birth to a horrible monstrosity.

3 The state of affairs in your home is not published in the newspapers but people can definitely read it on your face and in your eyes.

4 A woman will never have full possession of her husband until she has full possession of his mind.

5 There is no place like home as when you hold a receipt in your hand for the last payment on it.

6 A woman can overpower a man more quickly with her sex than with her cooking until he's past ninety-nine.

7 When you judge the other person by yourself you are exposing yourself to yourself.

8 For those who see a sunrise and a sunset there must inevitably be shadows in between that will come and go.

1 Fanatical dogmas will torture the mind of man until the light from a star just born a million light years distant will reach us.

2 Some folks don't like my epigrams because like a bug in a rug they hate to be spotlighted.

3 I have been accused of disturbing folk's peace of mind by disgruntling them, but how else could I make a fire almost out burn hot except by stirring the coals?

4 Sometimes a fellow will get bilious after satisfying his craving for something he had been wanting all his life.

5 Necessity puts fire under our feet and makes our fingers do double duty.

6 Vanity is not what most people think it is. It's making oneself believe in a lie.

7 A fellow's writing is like a fellow's checking account. It depends on the signature as to what he can draw on it.

8 Anger never takes time to declare war. It tears in with destructive and murderous intent.

1   You can never see your strength until
    you brush aside your weakness.

2   Disappointment always has Suicide trail-
    ing close behind him like a hungry lean
    wolf waiting for the master's voice to
    sic him on to someone fallen by the way-
    side.

3   Squabbling is nothing more nor less than
    two inferiority complexes in conflict with
    each other.

4   Woe unto the man that marries a woman
    who intends to fit him into her master
    plan.

5   An optimist will add up his column of
    years and always show a gain.

6   Hope is a beam of light that illuminates
    a fogged mind and drives fear into hid-
    ing.

7   Jealousy is an insidious rusting away
    process that destroys the mind and fills
    the heart with petty grievances.

8   Some folks like some ships at sea can
    take more battering than others before
    they break up.

1   You may think yourself a sly old fox because you are past thirty and still a bachelor but that is only because you have nothing a woman really wants.

2   Your actions, trivial as they may be, will reveal the state of your mind.

3   It is possible to fight overwhelming desires until one drops dead from exhaustion.

4   A grudge, as soon as it grows up, gives birth to a heap of little grudges.

5   Sometimes a fellow will run around with dogs even if his name isn't Fido.

6   Give yourself the acid test for purity and you will discover that you tarnish a little here and there.

7   Your heirs will tear apart bit by bit that for which you fought with years of your life to keep in one piece.

8   No one can feel for others as long as their senses are tuned to feel only for themselves.

9   You can, if you exert it sufficiently, make your mind pull you out of the rut after your hands and feet have failed to do it.

1 There are times when it is wise to put on mental blinkers so the only thing visible is the road ahead.

2 How do you know that the cinder in your eye didn't save your life by a split second because you pulled over to the curb to get it out and missed the car that would have collided with you?

3 If the girl is intellectual and you admit to yourself that you are not, you will lose your identity the day you marry her.

4 It's one thing to have a fault and another thing to nourish it.

5 A ton of fool's gold would keep a poor man wonderfully happy until he found out it was worthless.

6 Death snatches at our every breath like a youngster snatching for the gold ring as he whirls around on the merry-go-round.

7 A thing highly tempered always sounds the loudest, carries the farthest, vibrates the longest and snaps quickest.

1 The keener your taste is for sweet the the more bitter will be the taste of gall.

2 You can never sweep the cobwebs off your brain by sweeping the sky.

3 The tragedy of divorce lies in its wreckage.

4 The system of capitalism is to industry what the root system is to a productive tree.

5 There is a life factor in every element that environment brings into material animation and reproduction by a method impossible for our restricted intelligence to conceive.

6 A man tied to an overwhelming wife is like a dog on a chain. Both might get used to it after a while.

7 The dear old girls!—God bless their souls and their husbands their money bags.

8 A fellow's vision of happiness is like the horizon in that it's never where he thinks he sees it.

9 The only difference in your blood related son and daughter and the one you adopted is in your ego.

1 Poor folks are more likely to trust each other than rich folks because there is nothing poor folks can steal from each other worth the risk or the effort.

2 A man on stilts taking long strides will get to where he is going quickly if he doesn't bog down in the mud. A man with determination will also get there even if he has to build bridges over the mud on his way.

3 Rules and regulations like wagon wheels have a way of getting rusty and useless in the course of a generation.

4 In trying to outshine the other fellow you can become so blinding that everyone will turn their back to you.

5 Fear is a master with a whip that can strike with agonizing pain.

6 You can never retrieve a lost opportunity.

7 In the fact that you were born lies the proof that you possess an immortal spark of life.

8 Life is like marble in the hands of a sculptor. What he makes of it depends on his mood and ability.

1 Capital punishment is justifiable in the minds of most folks only as long as it's someone else's son who is to be hung.

2 If it were as difficult to darken a man's character as it is his eyes without getting hurt it isn't likely you would try darkening his character.

3 Some folks are like some nations, they set the price of peace so high no one can afford to pay it.

4 No matter what history records, there will always be those who will proofread it for errors.

5 A bird on the wing looking for insects in the air never sees the worm on the ground.

6 A social ladder when charm is lacking must always be a long golden ladder to reach the status aimed at.

7 We are all duty bound to forge at least one link in the chain of posterity and make that link an enduring one.

8 It matters not how gentle a man may be, he is still a beast of prey tearing and cutting a once living thing apart, to be eaten.

1 They say that lightning seldom strikes the same place twice. Opportunity is also like that.

2 Faith is like a floodlight because it reveals things enveloped in darkness that could not otherwise be seen.

3 A light heart unburdens heavily loaded shoulders.

4 You can never solve the solution of a problem with an alibi.

5 Living isn't life and by the same token life isn't living except when you are alive to it.

6 Your fair-weather friends will always hole in like rats in a manure pile when they see a threatening cloud coming your way.

7 A heart warming smile can thaw out a frozen face.

8 A house is only an assembly of wood, brick and stone and will never be a home until the folks within give it life and personality.

1   After all, why should youth worry about old age? Does a budding tree worry about the coming winter?

2   Gold can serve many a useful purpose but never to sleep on.

3   Sometimes the lips can put together that which the tongue dashed to bits.

4   Someone may destroy your confidence like a woodman with his axe a tree, but if the root of your confidence refuses to die, it will one day sprout forth with a new vigor to face the world again.

5   Fortune favors not the strong or the weak, the high born, nor the one of low birth, but the one who can recognize good fortune when he has it.

6   It's easy to yell advice to a man caught in a cross current while you stand safely on shore.

7   If you do someone a favor do it with a feeling that he would have done the same for you and not remembered it.

8   A person lacking confidence in himself is always certain the cards are stacked against him.

1   If a man tells you he would not want to relive life even if he could, he is telling you point blank that he never knew what living life is like.

2   Striving for an opportunity and then letting it go by is like laboring to make a clearing in a forest and then failing to plant and harvest.

3   You wouldn't think your neighbor could hate you for putting out the fire in his house while he was away, but he could —if he started the fire to collect insurance.

4   A man has executive ability when he hires only those who know how to run his business better than he can.

5   A thought is never free as long as it is in hiding.

6   There is strength in knowledge because it is fortified with certainty.

7   Patience is a condition of the mind, therefore one must first have a mind to condition.

8   How long you can hang onto the end of a rope high in mid-air depends on what you consider your life worth.

PART TWELVE

1　More often than not it's not the weight of the years that will kill a man but the weight around his middle.

2　The extent of your appreciation in getting what you always wanted will depend upon your age when you get it.

3　To understand youth you must understand a colt that refuses to be haltered or harnessed.

4　It all depends on how you look upon death. To an undertaker it is only a trade.

5　It could be that you convinced your wife so thoroughly before marriage how perfect she was that now she can't forget it.

1 You couldn't remove incompatibility where it exists even if you took the word out of every dictionary.

2 A writer's first book in a bookstore is like a nameless breed of dog in a kennel of pedigreed dogs. The dogs don't know the difference but the folks who buy them do.

3 An era like growing fruit must develop slowly to its maturity.

4 Death cannot frighten anyone who has nothing to lose by dying.

5 The only ones who can put strength in a law are the people who are supposed to observe and be obedient to it.

6 A fellow's troubles always look bigger and more complicated to him than to anyone else.

7 Love, like most perishable things, if kept lukewarm will soon sour and decay.

8 Life is like a rider on a bicycle who must always keep in mind the law of equilibrium to keep from taking a nasty fall.

9 Medicine from out of a bottle cannot cure frustration but initiative from within yourself can.

1 Some folks make themselves believe in a God because they are afraid not to.

2 A mistake can be like a shot from a cartridge scattering wide and striking an unintended bird on the wing nearby.

3 Will power can make you see what does not exist, hear when there is nothing to hear, and make you think you are what you are not.

4 When ambition is glowing hot, sparks are bound to fly.

5 Shortening pie crust makes it better but not so the day when there is a job to be done.

6 The tides run high and the tides run low and success rides its crest.

7 In the scientific sense, man developed a brain because he couldn't outrun or outclimb his enemies; he had to outsmart them.

8 Idle days shorten the calendar year.

9 Our dear Uncle Sam is very fair and considerate in his demands. He knows we can't take it with us and that our heirs will squander it fighting over their share.

1 Who originated income taxes? — The Democrats, back in 1893, and soon after they were declared unconstitutional by the Supreme Court.—Grandpa wants his money back.

2 Ambition—a fire that starts from a spark of desire and burns its way through all things that oppose it.

3 Ask a pessimist what sunlight is good for and he'll tell you, "To get a miserable sunburn."

4 Shortening will shorten piecrust and widen the man who eats it.

5 A man can love two women at the same time when each has what the other lacks that he would prefer all in one.

6 You can never distill the essence of truth from anything but pure undiluted truth.

7 Some folks claim they can read their future with tea leaves while others know they can read it in the eyes of a loved one.

8 Smoke coming out of a chimney is not always an indication of a fire in the hearth. It could be the smoke from personalities clashing.

1 Facts remain facts no matter how much you profane or rose-color them.

2 The trouble with most folks looking for happiness and not finding it is that they must find the seed first and then cultivate it to maturity.

3 There are those who proclaim themselves an enemy to everything in which they cannot profit.

4 Vice, like a contagious disease, never remains confined to the location of infection and is therefore of public interest to eradicate it.

5 It is in the nature of some folks to trample on flower beds which they did not plant.

6 Beware of people whose feelings cannot be hurt because they can hurt you without being conscious of the fact.

7 For some folks life is like a flame clinging to a candlewick and burning brightest just before it burns out.

8 It takes much more than a bank balance to keep home life on the credit side of the ledger.

1 When memory plays on our heartstrings the ghosts of yesterday come forth from their graves and sit solemnly by our side.

2 Poverty's only asset is the fact that it never causes death from overeating.

3 A big heart always takes on big burdens.

4 It is true that a woman never forgets her sex but it is also true that no man wants her to forget it.

5 Once upon a time a farmer lived in a dell. Today he lives on his yacht because the nearby city awakened with a yawn, stretched and moved in on him.

6 All through life we walk in lockstep with our inner self, one or the other occasionally stepping ahead and taking over the lead.

7 There is strength in unity, but so also is there strife in proportion to the numbers that make up the union.

8 The importance of a thing depends on how close one is to his grave.

9 A person may be loaded with acquired principal and yet possess no principle whatsoever.

1 Some folks are like a match that burns out before it starts the fire under the kettle.

2 An idler run out of money considers his watch his most useless possession and will invariably hock it first.

3 The thing you strive for is never out of reach until a coffin lid is between you and that thing.

4 If you believe that God created man first and then created a woman from the rib of that man, then you must believe He did so to inflate the ego of the male. If you think of a man as a stuffed shirt, remember, he came by it honestly.

5 Like most folks, an egg never goes bad on one side without involving the other side also.

6 An expensive wife and expensive shoes must both wear well to be worth the high price paid for them.

7 It is doubtful if any sane man would let his worst enemy drown if he could save him.

8 Timing is the important thing. Men and nations live or die because of it.

1 History, to be truthful, must be unbiased and written without personal emotion. Such a writer never existed and never will.

2 Credit is like a pair of good feet. Without them one cannot go anywhere except on crutches.

3 A beautiful woman without warmth is like a beautiful stove lacking glowing coals on a cold night.

4 Experience, not common sense, is the master mind.

5 If you must tag a thing you are giving with a sigh of regret, better that you don't give it.

6 Many play the game of life like they play cards. They bluff all the way.

7 You can't slow down the footsteps of Time chasing after you but you can certainly run like hell to keep it from catching up with you before you get to your goal.

8 Too often the desires of youth are not attained until one no longer has the sense of emotion to be thrilled by them.

1 To a petty person the petty things in life are always the most outstanding.

2 Where there can be a profit there can also be a loss, in marriage, in being single or on the stock exchange.

3 Your servant first considers herself an underdog when she comes to the conclusion that you are a bitch.

4 Humans are like wine, sweet, sour, intoxicating, cold, flat, and some produce a murderous headache.

5 Any man capable of robbing you by conniving is capable of cutting your throat while you are asleep.

6 Beware of Futility, he's a high powered salesman out to sell you his bitterish herbs and fruits.

7 Breaking up your home because you don't like the looks of things is like breaking your mirror because you don't like what you see in it.

8 No man likes hard labor but he is fortunate indeed if he can get himself to believe he does.

1 Human nature varies with the seasons and reasons.

2 A woman may forgive a man for infidelity but she will never forget it as long as she is in love with him.

3 Fame is like a candle light. It burns bright and with vigor as long as there is wax to feed it.

4 When circumstances make a servant the master, he invariably becomes a greater snob than the master ever was.

5 Never condemn other folks' children until after you have spent your own last seed of reproduction.

6 Elbow grease is a substance produced by your mind for the purpose of oiling your working joints.

7 A man's mind is like a copper piece. It takes endless polishing to keep it bright.

8 Sometimes an excuse is so lame it needs crutches to support it.

9 May God reward the farmer who speeds his tractor so that the farmer may reward the firm that made it and the firm that made it reward the bank that financed it.

1 A stomach at peace with itself makes for a man at peace with the world.

2 Don't offer your shoulder to the wheel if you don't intend to strain yourself.

3 The world will applaud a counterfeit if spotlighted and ignore a masterpiece under a dim light.

4 A man remembering his youth is never impatient with youth.

5 A house can be cold even though the room temperature is hot enough to set it on fire.

6 When the world focuses its eyes on a man it does so for selfish reasons. He is expected to do one of two things, make the world a better place to live in or worse than it has ever been.

7 Your bluff will look more realistic if you live extravagantly on a bluff.

8 Some folks like to clutter up their minds with trash like they do their attics.

9 Like dice, life is a scramble of circumstances—win or lose.

1 The world is a spherical prison on which we are confined for life, rotating furiously to keep us dizzy so we can't think about it.

2 Most folks die without ever paying the debt they owe themselves.

3 Why bargain with yourself over your every need? — Your heirs won't bargain while spending your money.

4 You can't deny the natural law of compensation. First man makes the clothes, then clothes make the man.

5 Betting on anything that carries with it the risk of losing is like putting money in a pocket that has a hole in it and betting you won't lose it.

6 Bad government sires poverty and poverty sires bad government — a vicious circle.

7 A book that is popular keeps itself alive and incidentally the author.

8 Accept with noble good sense the grunting at you of a hog if he's responsible for your comfort.

PART THIRTEEN

1 You must first buy experience before you can sell it and make a profit.

2 Actually, your watch dog guards his own home and incidentally yours.

3 Youth is old age in the budding stage.

4 Heaven might shield you against an invasion but it's safer to rely on guns.

5 An egotist is one who thinks the earth was made for him to stand on and the sun to keep him warm.

6 With some folks, the discredits in their make up seep out occasionally. In others it is forever gushing out.

1   Life lives on the dying pain of those it consumes.

2   You can't abbreviate, give and take without cheating or being cheated.

3   It is true that when a man says, "I am holier than thou," he is holier indeed—in the head.

4   The moment a secret acquires a mate it is no longer a secret.

5   Fame is definitely a product of publicity. Both live and die as one.

6   Folks who can't find a gain in adding up their experiences are indeed poor mathematicians.

7   If an infant remembered all of his injuries he would grow up to be an incurable coward.

8   Somewhere beyond the visible horizon, the radiance of a coming civilization is trying to break through darkening clouds heavily saturated with intolerance and hate.

9   Necessity is a hermaphrodite, being both the mother of invention and the father of crime.

1 Be honest, at least to yourself. Would you give a merchant his dollar back if he gave you one too many in change?

2 A frustrated career woman will roast to a crispy brown in the radiance of her husband's success.

3 A lightheaded person always thinks he can reach his goal gliding to it on air like a bird on the wing.

4 Ordinarily I would say, you can't eat your cake and have it too but I know men who will swear they keep theirs a deuce of a long time after eating a piece their wife baked.

5 All of us are inescapable prisoners of our mind and hog-tied to conventions.

6 A grudge will scatter and cultivate the seeds from which revenge will sprout.

7 Man and wife sometimes become commonplace to each other taking for granted that they will always be where they are like the heirloom on their shelf.

8 To solve a problem one must first understand the problem.

1 When your school chums begin to die out one by one it's high time you stopped scrimping and saving for the future.

2 No one is likely to see your one big fault if you keep it covered with enough little attributes.

3 Your mind can make an indistinct voice behind a wall hear what it wants your ears to hear.

4 Folks who feel disappointment keenly always see failure lurking in every under-taking.

5 Only busy bees of one sort or another can make honey or money.

6 There definitely is such a thing as a pessimistic cold. You catch the chill by getting too close to a pessimist.

7 When you are not wanted any time is the wrong time.

8 If you stayed with it and succeeded folks will say that you were lucky. But if it died on your hands they will say, "An obstinate fool such as you are had it coming—I told you so."

1 The indisputable law of nature that only the most fit shall survive is also true in business and at the work bench.

2 Fame, when it dies, does so in agonizing torture.

3 The difference between the desire to scribble and the desire to scratch depends on whether your fingers itch or your back itches.

4 A fool has two needs. Another fool and himself.

5 You can't see cleanliness looking through a dirty window or a depraved mind.

6 Money can make your heart sing and violins play.

7 As long as man strives for the most favorable striking positions just so long will war threaten.

8 The only thing alarming about an alarm clock is that it won't go off when it's supposed to.

9 Things will be worse tomorrow unless you make them better today.

10 A welcome mat outside one's door does not necessarily mean the same thing inside.

1 Hesitation will knock Opportunity cold everytime it sees it.

2 Everyone enjoyed the picnic in the park except those who had to clean up after you.

3 Fun and laughter is natural to the young. Oldsters must produce it synthetically.

4 Civilization rides on wheels and so do its victims.

5 You can't turn the hands of time forward with impatience.

6 The meek know their strength only in unity.

7 Love fires ambition—dissension cools it —divorce freezes it.

8 A guilty conscience always tries to elude the mind.

9 You can start a helluva big fire with a marriage license.

10 A man is his own master until the little woman greets him at the door with a kiss or a frying pan. It matters not which. The end result is the same.

1   Old fools brag about the richness of time not realizing that it will be the accumulation of time that will bury them.

2   Nothing suffers agony like a dying hope.

3   The day cannot be young and gay if the heart is not that way.

4   What does the world gain by hanging a man or killing a sparrow? Whatever they did came naturally to both.

5   A good epigram can be likened to a good glue in that both can mend a weakness, a break, or a thing about to fall apart.

6   No man or government is your master as long as you are free to leave them.

7   Revenge may be sweet but the fruit it bears is horribly bitter.

8   If your mind is tuned only to the past you are no longer present.

9   In all of nature, the Bloom of Youth is matchless.

10 Abruptness, little man, does not build up your importance—it tears you down to the level of things that crawl.

1   Fear on your mind can drown you just as easily as a millstone around your neck.

2   There can be a delightful kernel of character within regardless of one's exterior appearance as witness the prickly burr surrounding the chestnut.

3   Trying to run away from yourself is like a dog chasing after his tail. It's always ahead of him.

4   You can frighten an opportunity away by snatching for it too eagerly.

5   Experience is the saponifying agent of trial and error which in the change becomes knowledge.

6   With some folks, their likes and dislikes of a thing depend on what they had to pay for it.—Marriage included.

7   It takes courage for someone to swat you on the nose but none for you to swat him back.

8   A woman should never marry a man because she loves the color of his money or the color of his hair because the chances are he will eventually lose both.

1   My philosophy of "work hard" has made me three fortunes so far. Follow it and maybe you'll make at least one—then spend it before you lose it.

2   An accumulation of years is not an asset but the experience gained while accumulating them is.

3   You can't satisfy an ugly tempered dog with lovely words when what he wants is a lovely bone.

4   Some folks' sense of value is limited to what a nickel will buy.

5   There are other ways than a Turkish bath that can steam a fellow up.

6   Life is built on the indisputable fact that it must destroy life to survive.

7   Civilization has become highly complex —division of labor and collaboration of nation with nation must of necessity become an integral part of it in order to survive.

8   Body and soul are like lifelong friends who hate the thought of parting.

1 Character is like molten ore, its purity and strength being dependent upon its refinement.

2 There is much beyond the limit of sight and sound which is mysterious and will forever remain so because the human mind lacks the necessary senses to detect, penetrate or analyze them.

3 The passion of old folks is like a damp match that won't ignite without a lot of coaxing.

4 To the blacksmith it is common knowledge to forge only while the iron is hot.

5 Only a foolish hen cackles over every egg it lays believing that every one will hatch.

6 Poverty is not a disgrace but it's very, very inconvenient.

7 Pure essence of truth when applied to a sore spot can react like vitriolic acid.

8 Heredity molded the child—mothers and teachers must mold the man.

9 Success should come only to those who can take it without becoming obnoxious.

1 A man's interpretations of love change with the years, the seasons and reasons.

2 It is a fact that your disposition can dis-position you.

3 In the process of aging the tendency is for the good characteristics to get better and the bad ones to get worse.

4 Nothing in life is really real except the moments of pain and the moments of pleasure.

5 To every human being comes the day of reckoning. Some folks blind themselves to the loss column while others just don't give a damn.

6 Never spur a spirited horse or a spirited husband—both can kick up an awful fuss.

7 Your wife or girl friend will pay you more for your lovely poem than any editor ever will.

8 Instinct can outtalk reason and lull the conscience to sleep.

9 Raking a person over the coals will turn him to a crispy brown and will also turn him bitter.

1 Nature insists that we die by the time we're fifty and inflicts us with torturesome aches and pains for our disobedience.

2 A hole in one's pocket isn't the only way one can lose his money.

3 Winter with its ice and snow will settle upon one's roof and land but never in the heart or on the mind if love is there to keep it away.

4 Ambition is like a mirage because the insight sees what it wants to see before the thing strived for becomes a reality.

5 A man can love his wife and children with his heart and soul and yet—he can love himself better.

6 Human nature is basically the same in all of us, it's the way we apply it in our daily living that makes us all different.

7 He who owns no silver but sees the silver lining in every cloud is abundantly wealthy.

8 Some folks' sense of reasoning would be better if they stood on their head and let their feet do the thinking for them.

1 Would you consider your so-called friend still your friend if he refused to guarantee payment on your note so you could borrow money at the bank?

2 Death and Eternity go hand in hand forever.

3 It is a waste of effort to sharpen a bread knife when there is no bread in the house.

4 Concentration is a third eye that sees what the normal eyes see not.

5 Quoting prayer verbiage by the mile does not make you religious, not even mildly so. But side stepping a thing alive at your feet does.

6 In the war between Truth and Deceit, Truth is invariably outmaneuvered.

7 If you ask one hundred successful men to sum up the secret of success put into a single sentence the answer would be, "Put in more hours and live with your chosen work until you are big enough and financially strong enough to delegate some of your work to others."

1   In my subconscious inspirations and inclinations I suspect that my mind is not my own but merely a link in a chain reaching far back to my prehistoric ancestors.

2   Human beings are like budding flowers at your feet. They will never mature to what Nature intended them to be as long as they are stepped on.

3   Why waste your breath trying to educate someone to your way of thinking when you can have more fun blowing bubbles?

4   Couples can certainly find more enjoyable ways of expending their energy than in fighting personalities.

5   Silverware and impeccable table manners do not change the human beast of prey from what he is.

6   The God you seek is within you and can be found only in the depth of your heart.

7   Unrecognized talent is like a Bird of Paradise. You've got to travel far and suffer many hardships in unfriendly forests before you can capture it and mount it in a display case for all the world to see and admire.

1 Whatever it may be, a cautious person will analyze it while a suspicious one will condemn it.

2 Procrastination is a twin brother to Alibi.

3 You can't sell yourself a lie that you don't care as long as your heart laughs back at you mockingly and says, "Who do you think you are fooling?"

4 Only Hate can kill Love and only Death can kill Hate.

5 Throw caution to the wind and one day the wind will come back to get what's left of you.

6 Dishonesty has crooked feet than can't walk a straight line.

7 Happiness can only be maintained by a heart that feeds it.

8 Even if you were raised in a barn your present home need not look and smell like one.

9 If you and your competitor keep grinding axes in full view of each other, sooner or later one of you will get chopped down.

PART FOURTEEN

1   It's really tough on a fellow when his girl friend raises a stink and insists on a new mink every time she sees his wife with a new one.

2   Only feet that move stumble.

3   The unattainable is no farther away than an inch beyond the reach of your mind.

4   Some folks like some trees just can't take new root to re-establish themselves once they are moved.

5   Pity the simpleton who thinks the stars were made to twinkle for his enjoyment.

1 Everyone carries his heaven and hell within him all the days of his life.

2 You just can't step out of line as long as your conscience guides you.

3 Folks who magnify petty grievances to the size of a mountain will sooner or later find themselves buried under the weight of them.

4 Some folks actually never woke up after they were born. You see them on every highway.

5 Sooner or later even an eagle flying high must come down to earth.

6 Nature is the ultimate in cruel savagery. She maims, kills and eats alive everything she brings into being.

7 Within every mind there is a graveyard wherein each and every one secretly buries his heartaches and disappointments.

8 There are many varieties of sponges on the ocean beds of the world but only one variety that comes to your home.

9 No one faith has a monopoly on righteousness or superstition.

1   Some day in the distant future men will cure the cause of crime instead of taking revenge on it.

2   Falling in love is like falling in quicksand. The longer you're in it the less chance of escape.

3   Taste is governed by discrimination not reason.

4   Marriage adds nothing to the zest of living. It only legalizes a privilege.

5   There is only slight difference between a religious contribution and the premium paid on fire insurance. Both are intended to insure against fire.

6   Don't tell your friend everything you know until you know he's your friend.

7   Come on! Cheer up! The doctor who said it might be dead before you are.

8   Why stand with your mouth agape at the mention of a third sex? Nature has, is now and will forever experiment.

9   Every devil has a million secretaries fulfilling his orders.

1   The tide of fortune in the lives of men, like the ocean tide, is forever at the mercy of circumstances.

2   The element of time is the same to the infant who died at birth as it is to the centenarian who lies in his coffin at the age of one hundred.

3   Humanity cannot be enslaved except in an atmosphere of deceit.

4   A rich man is forever in a quandary not knowing who loves him for his money or for himself.

5   Some women are like blue-white diamonds—brilliant, expensive and cold.

6   Fear is definitely born in your mind and when fully grown hibernates into your feet.

7   The only difference between ancient history and modern is in the distance of observation. Human nature is always the same.

8   Only today belongs to you. The future is reserved for those yet unborn.

1 On what does one base his superiority? Color, club affiliations, title, wealth? Take notice, my good friend—the lowly worm looking for his lady love in the hollow of your skull will know none of these things.

2 No one ever benefits from a wedding feast except the caterers and moochers.

3 Every man who hangs his hat on the hatrack in a barber shop demonstrates his faith in humanity.

4 If the spark of life could see the struggles of man prior to birth, few indeed would choose to be born if asked.

5 Sentimentalists can say what they wish, but the fact is, a male bird singing to his lady bird does so to display his ego not to entertain her.

6 My idea of a contented man is one who has everything he wants, but I am certain no such man exists.

7 A point of view is like seeing a sunrise or sunset. How it looks to you depends on your mood, age and from where you observe it.

1 Snap judgment is good judgment only when nothing can be lost or gained either way.

2 Of what use is life when you are not conscious of living it?

3 An idea is never any good unless in some way you can cash in on it.

4 Every egotist has at least one redeeming characteristic. He'll fight with tooth and nail to prove he's as good as he says he is.

5 Centuries do not change the philosophies of life but the people who live in it do.

6 A restraining ball and chain to which a person may be helplessly chained is not necessarily visible to the eye.

7 The cure for frustration never came from a whiskey bottle.

8 Some folks are capable of closing their ears to annoying sounds and their eyes to glaring faults.

9 You are likely to live longer by being overcautious but you'll never get as much fun out of living as you would if you weren't.

1 The most delightful spots are always the most difficult to get to.

2 Every human being is like a clock. Some run good, some run bad, and some need winding up more often than others.

3 There is an unwritten law between bores that they must listen to each other—but they don't.

4 Some men put their wives on a pedestal in the presence of others and then kick the base out from under them as soon as they are by themselves.

5 Every human on earth is a blood linked relative to every other human in the chain of evolution.

6 Youth always bypasses those who were born old.

7 You can't taste the sweet in honey if it's too liberally mixed with gall.

8 An oyster lives its entire life in its shell. Some folks live that way too.

9 Unused tables and such things are not the only places where dust and cobwebs collect.

1 You can win a race on crutches if your mind can outrun your opponent's feet.

2 Overcaution is a millstone around the neck of Progress.

3 Folks trying to rid themselves of a torturesome burden on their back are like a dog with a cat firmly entrenched on its back trying desperately to shake it off as it runs wildly hell-bent.

4 You can't get power from the mainspring in yourself or in your watch if you don't wind them up.

5 Some parents become aware of their own shortcomings only after they crop out in their offspring.

6 The difference between working on a job and slaving at it is in the pay.

7 For a thing to be vitally important to you, you must crave it.

8 With man's reasoning faculty as it is at this stage of evolution, he has no alternative but to conclude that life is complex, that all of life is made up of two separate functioning forces incapable of material existence except by mutual cohesion and collaboration.

1 To some folks, honesty and fair play is a religion while to others it is only sentimental foolishness.

2 Sooner or later everyone misses hitting the nail on the head and whacks his thumb painfully.

3 Like the horizon, the end of your world is not where it seems to be.

4 You can never get a heavily loaded wagon out of a mudhole by tugging at it halfheartedly.

5 When so-called justice takes a man's life, it isn't justice, it's revenge.

6 If you can't relieve a man of his burden you can at least keep it lightened by not reminding him of it.

7 An optimist will side glance his misery while a pessimist will examine it under a microscope.

8 A once happy marriage that has cooled is like yesterday's embers in the hearth that has lost its warmth and glow but still retains a spark that could ignite with a little coaxing.

1 You don't have to have your teeth pulled out just because you can't give them enough to chew on.

2 Pull an ungrateful person out of a rut and he'll never give up trying to figure out what you gained by it.

3 The moment some fellows get to thinking you love them like a brother they move right in on you.

4 Some folks run after Opportunity until they lose their wind when as a matter of fact Opportunity is panting for air running after them.

5 Today boy meets girl—tomorrow he meets her bills.

6 The more anxious a girl is to wrangle out a proposal the harder she feigns she's hard to get.

7 Testing the strength of your heart against your mind in a tug of war can prove fatal to your well-being.

8 What man wouldn't give up every shoe he owns and then some to be a barefoot boy again?

9 Life hangs on a thread and so does one's fortune.

1 Frustration is a highly contagious disease that one catches by being in close proximity to others who already have it.

2 A supercautious man always makes certain his girl friend uses the same color and brand of lipstick his wife does.

3 An employer will pay you more for your know-how than he will for your sweat.

4 Stolen food is hard on the digestive system because the mind is not at ease while consuming it.

5 A mouse when in danger will scamper for its hole and stay there whereas your fear will scamper to your feet and stimulate them into action.

6 Politics like a meandering stream stays clean until someone stirs up the mud at the bottom.

7 Most folks can see and appreciate beauty but only an artist can feel it emotionally and interpret it.

8 Sometimes the thing we seek is so close to us our eyes overlook it.

1   A mad dog can't be trusted—neither can neighbors or governments mad at each other.

2   There are more folks allergic to irritating temperaments than to irritating weeds.

3   To live righteously is to compromise with yourself and with others who also claim the right to live.

4   Give away your yesterdays to your memory but keep every living moment of today for yourself.

5   Some folks never relax their face until death does it for them.

6   When you propose marriage to your girl friend remember that you are all in one breath proposing marriage to her whole family.

7   Profit in business is not necessarily a reflection of brilliance in personnel and neither does loss reflect stupidity—circumstantial timing plays the leading role either way.

1   Never stir live coals near an open keg of dynamite unless you are prepared for the consequences.

2   Sometimes the hands want what the eyes see but the mind won't let them have it.

3   Every day should be Mother's Day except payday—payday should belong to father.

4   If you want to know what your girl friend is likely to be like twenty years hence—look her mother over carefully when she doesn't know you are around.

5   You can't escape Old Man Responsibility tagging along behind you by hiding in the shadow of a whiskey glass.

6   There is no such thing as a humane war because every war is based on injury and bloodletting.

7   No one has a right to expect more from the other fellow than from himself unless he is paying the other fellow at least as much as he considers himself worth.

8   A wolf at the door will scare pennies into hiding.

1　To be helpful one must first know that person's needs.

2　I am certain no one would object to criticism if the critic would at all times keep before him his own shortcomings.

3　Foul characters have no sense of smell —if they did they would try to run away from themselves.

4　An oiled tongue will skid dangerously in inclement weather.

5　A turtle in one way at least is wiser than man—it supports a home no larger than its requirements.

6　Not all the little devils are in hell. Sometimes you can see them in a woman's eyes.

7　Instinct has a way of making you obey or pay.

8　A grouch always carries a pained expression on his face from the burden of the chip on his shoulder.

9　Difficulties when mastered should add up a profit.

1 No man is actually an individual—he's the total sum and substance of his ancestors.

2 A receptive ear belonging to a sympathetic listener can make one's troubles shrink to insignificance.

3 A luxury ceases to be a luxury when it becomes a burden.

4 Some folks are called bores because they drill the brain.

5 Inconsiderate words weigh heavy like a millstone and are just as capable of crushing and pulverizing.

6 Every person in a casket is a pauper.

7 Fear contaminates with bitters the thing coveted and stolen.

8 Only foolish women believe that every engagement ring is inseparably paired with a wedding ring.

9 A hobby is a criminal waste of time to one who has none.

10 Cars are not the only things with an overdrive. Some folks are also built that way.

1   There are two ways to get rich quick. One way is to rob a bank. The better way is to marry the widow that owns the bank.

2   All folks are like a clock of one sort or another. Some run fast and some run slow and some you just can't make run at all.

3   There is a challenge in every breath and and a victory won in every day of living.

4   An epigram lacks sense of reasoning if there has been no personal experience to which it can be applied.

5   Some members of a family love to loan money to other members of the family so they can talk about it and gloat.

6   Sleepy little towns sometimes hear the voice of destiny and wake up.

7   Never let your mind express itself when your tongue is in flames.

8   In my opinion the life cycle is nothing more nor less than chemical compounds in animation, be it in the ground, above the ground or in the depth of the ooze at the bottom of the seas.

PART FIFTEEN

1   A fly settling on your nose can alter the course of your life by exposing your true nature to those near you.

2   You can abuse authority by inflating it.

3   It's really funny how poison ivy can drag your best and your worst characteristics right out from under your skin.

4   On more than one occasion my castles in the sky collapsed and buried my dreams under the rubble.

5   You can't get along with others until you first learn how to get along with yourself.

1 A good swimmer does not fear deep water because he has confidence in himself.

2 You can never think clearly through a frightened mind.

3 A woman's nervous system is more intricate than the maize of wires in a television set that most of us will never understand—either the woman or the set.

4 By trying too hard to safeguard your future, you can lose your grip on the present.

5 Why magnify the other fellow's faults when you are so close to your own that you can see so well without magnification.

6 If you haven't the courage to face your own problems, you have no right to direct someone else from a safe distance as to how they should face theirs.

7 You can't fight off a rhino with a fly swatter—neither can you, fear.

8 The danger in marrying your sweetheart lies in the fact that your children might steal her affection from you.

1   A positive pitch can sell anything to a negative mind.

2   If you want to succeed the boss, think and do as he does. That's the way he got where he is.

3   There is a painful longing in the heart of almost every man for the things he was once certain would be—now knowing never will be.

4   Backward folks detest competition—progressive ones invite it.

5   Negative thinking brings negative results.

6   Persistence can ultimately wear down resistance like a grindstone will wear down steel.

7   Some men think they always do as they please when as a matter of fact, their wives had already made the decision for them.

8   Trouble is always on the lookout for people who anticipate it.

9   Nothing is likely to last forever except your debts.

1 Even though you never acquired a financial legacy or ever expect to—take heart —you may have acquired it in your physical make up and temperament.

2 You can never hope to fathom the mind because its bottom rests on the mire of antiquity.

3 Life is like so much modeling clay— what one does with it depends on one's insight, imagination, desire and ability.

4 Inclination has a thousand eyes—education only two.

5 If your home was on fire, would you think of conserving your drinking water?

6 Live today—tomorrow is not yet born.

7 No sensible person wants a fight—but if someone socked that sensible person on the nose, it is very likely he would hit back with all his might.

8 From statistics gathered, I found that folks prefer to work themselves to death rather than worry themselves to death.

9 More likely than not, it was your mind that put the lines on your face—not the years.

1 Two brothers beat each other painfully arguing as to which one of them should inherit Betsy, the prize cow owned by their old bachelor Uncle Amos. The cow died before Amos did.

2 Even a good dog might bite once in a while, but a mad dog will bite at every opportunity.

3 A negative mind invariably hatches a negative reason for failure.

4 Nobility is not a specific blood type and therefore carries no right of distinction.

5 When a woman dotes over her husband it's a good indication she is not after his insurance.

6 Your friends—if they are your friends—will never believe what those who dislike you say about you even though what they say is true.

7 A troublesome wife is like a troublesome automobile—it depends on just how long your patience holds out before you decide to get a new one.

8 It isn't the color of a horse that makes him a champion.

1 Some old timers will never go into their second childhood because they never matured out of their first.

2 Sometimes a verbal bite gets infected and refuses to heal.

3 Don't chew on fat if it gives you indigestion.

4 At eighty miles per hour, Death has a grip on one side of the steering wheel while Luck has a grip on the other side.

5 There are those who always keep their nose to the wind hoping to smell out an argument.

6 Because nature considers life so lightly in the process of evolution, I have come to the conclusion that the life process is merely a commutation of chemical substances from one chemical to another, the spark of life being merely the fuse that ignites the process into action.

7 Frustration is an infection of defeatism.

8 Far beyond human understanding buried under the immensity of time and space lies the secret of all that is.

1 The wise accept life for what it is—the foolish build illusions around it.

2 It matters not what—every morning is a good morning as long as your feet are in your shoes instead of in a coffin.

3 In his eyes there was instinctive hate—not because he knew the man—but because he did not know him.

4 Some folks climbed up the ladder of evolution—some just stood still—and others never heard of the word.

5 Too often folks who get caught in the upper floors of a burning building jump out of a window and get killed—they might have at least waited until the fire was at their heels—who knows—they might have been saved.

6 A pot you watch will be slow to boil—a man you watch will be fast to steal.

7 War is an infection in the mind of humanity.

8 You will never gain a thing by refusing to face a bully, a creditor or a problem.

9 The world has a sole as big as its heart—as heavy and as crushing.

1 Maybe the elephant does know her strength but will allow the little man on her neck to rule her because she loves him.

2 Not everyone needs to stand on his head to see how topsy-turvy the world is.

3 You can drown in a puddle of fear even if the puddle is only imaginary.

4 A man whose wife supports him is always an expert economist and knows all the reasons for business failures.

5 Why should you worry—even the great and mighty Pharohs quit worrying about their dynasties thousands of years ago.

6 Everyone would like to be happy but not everyone is willing to contribute the ingredients necessary to its conclusion.

7 When a home ceases to be a home it becomes a workhouse.

8 Wasting a man's time or stealing his money is one and the same moral crime.

9 A speedy training in shoplifting for children is for the parents to show them how.

1 Admittedly dead crabs smell bad but assuredly, live ones are far worse by the irritation they set up.

2 Idleness for the old is a reward—for the the young it is a curse.

3 A shallow mind breeds hate because it has no depth of understanding.

4 There is a hacksaw of a sort for every chain that keeps one bound.

5 A yellow streak in the hair does not indicate a yellow streak in the mental make up.

6 Never let the bogy man scare you until you can actually put your finger on him.

7 From out of the boundless whirling atomic dust of antiquity came forth creatures endowed with life and intelligence— what is life and intelligence anyway?

8 Partnerships usually start with good intentions but too often end in distrust and dissension.

9 Woman—a two-legged species of mammal that thinks herself superior to man and is forever trying hard to prove it.

1   Regardless of reason or truth, you are a monster in the eyes of all who despise you.

2   In raw nature you will find many instances in which the mother becomes a a cannibal feast for her own brood.

3   You have no right to lay claim to a bit of this world unless you contribute something to its maintenance.

4   A bottle of miracle pills in a dying man's hand always gives Death the jitters.

5   Some women are too darn practical. They insist that Henry, Mike or Joe could reduce his waistline faster by pushing a vacuum cleaner instead of riding a bike before breakfast.

6   You will never show a gain by capitalizing your weakness.

7   In the melody of your love for her you will find the gigantic secret for your being.

8   The difference between being sensible and being practical is in the way you spend your money.

9   The less one's ambition, the more time that one has for leisure.

1 The worst thing about a fault is that it seldom stops growing.

2 What good will it do you to see what is behind you if you can't make use of what you see in front of you?

3 Fighting two opponents at one time is like fighting two problems at one time— one or the other can somehow manage to climb on your back from behind you and give you a painful shellacking.

4 It matters not how big and strong a ship may be—it takes know-how to keep it from dashing to bits on the rocks.

5 They were sure they could live on love before they were married and they proved it during the depression.

6 I knew a fellow once who could count to a thousand in ten languages. But I never could see what good it did him because he never could count a hundred dollars of his own in any language.

7 White washing an ugly tempered dog does not change his disposition.

8 Conscious life is only a momentary whistle-stop between the beginning of our life-line and its dead-end.

1   If the little girl playing with her doll habitually scolds it—beware you young gentlemen—she is certain to grow up to be an habitual scold.

2   Fighting with yourself always involves innocent bystanders.

3   You will never find perfection in Progress because it is riddled and scarred with trials and errors.

4   Too much of anything is unhealthy—especially poverty.

5   Pinheads think that to be a good executive they must scream their fool heads off by raising bloody hell with everyone around them.

6   Luxuries are an overabundance of necessities.

7   Every bogy man is a problem—to every problem there is an answer.

8   As long as necessity compels you to look at a price tag, you are not eligible for retirement.

9   If you made big, lived big, lost big and never shrunk to insignificance, you are still big.

1   The will to live derives its desire from instinct not necessarily from compensation as a direct result of living.

2   I've bet money on men and I've bet money on horses. I lost oftener on men than I did on horses.

3   Security is an illusion because death can make it useless.

4   If you carry your head too high you are liable to fall in a rut and break your neck.

5   You can never cover up your shortcomings with an argument.

6   Don't create problems for your employer —prevent them—he'll live longer and so will your job.

7   After fifty every birthday has at least one compensation—there won't be another one for a whole year.

8   A wonderful sweetheart doesn't necessarily make a wonderful wife.

9   A woman will put her best foot forward only when she has on her best shoes.

10 A knife can cut the hand that sharpened it.

1   A crop of nothing begets a crop of nothing.

2   The mind that refuses to face reality will soon enough face extinction.

3   Every million dollars carries a price tag.

4   Marriage is a swindle. Every community keeps the cost of a license down to a few bucks trying to make the male think that a wife is a cheap article.

5   Some folks are always certain they are going to lose the fight even though the fight is scheduled months ahead and the opponent might be dead by then.

6   Time will be with you or against you, depending on whether you are trying to save it or kill it.

7   A dog will not attack you if he knows you have a club in your hand held behind you.

8   Everyone utters at least two complaints in the course of his lifetime. He objects to coming and he objects to going.

9   Life gives us a stick of candy. Death takes it away from us long before we had time to enjoy it fully.

1 Whatever it is a rodent thinks when he finds himself trapped, so also does the mind of man think when he finds himself in a like predicament.

2 Sooner or later old age will claim your entire physical being—but that doesn't mean you must throw in your mind for good measure.

3 Only a small minority have the gift to be important without being obnoxious.

4 The strong should sustain the weak but not when they overburden you by climbing on your back while you are in a swirling current swimming for your life.

5 A loan to a friend can be likened to a life belt. It can support him until he is firmly established on his feet.

6 I used to get aggravated at people's stupid mistakes until it dawned on me that I was no exception.

7 Dame Fortune is like any beautiful woman who for some special reason will smile at some and frown at others.

8 Call it by any name you like, a bureaucratic government sooner or later becomes a tyrannical government.

1 It requires more than one player to play the game of fairplay.

2 A few men know instinctively how to succeed—the rest must learn how by trial and error.

3 The element of chance can make you or break you.

4 A worm born in a horse radish was certain during its entire life that there was nothing sweeter or better in all the world than a horse radish.

5 Why drive yourself crazy?—Take it easy, you'll get to the insane asylum soon enough.

6 Adaptation is a blood brother to specialization.

7 If you ran a race and won it, don't give your feet all the credit—remember that timing and co-ordination helped your feet win it.

8 Enthusiasm gives strength to every project.

9 George Bernard Shaw was born a wit. I acquired my wit by name.

1   More often than not, instinct not reasoning is at the control levers of our actions.

2   Life is a riddle and the answer is incased in death.

3   The frightfulness of the bogy man you think you see is always in proportion to the depth of your fears.

4   Self-love and Selfishness are identical twins even to the same fingerprints.

5   A strong mind rejects fear—a weak one soaks it up like a dry sponge.

6   It's a waste of energy to force a hand that has nothing in it.

7   You don't bark at a dog do you? Then why is it you bark at people?

8   Divorce lays an egg which starts hatching the same day a man's wife stops being his sweetheart.

9   There is a greater chance of escape from shackled feet than there is from a shackled mind.

10 Necessity is cold blooded and lawless. It knows no God, restrictions, law or order. History proves it.

1   Had it ever occurred to you that when you bought on credit terms you actually borrowed the money with which to buy it?

2   Life is useless while not in use.

3   When the heavy foot of Legal Right steps on the toe of Common Right—look out —because anything can happen.

4   There will be times when you'll be away ahead if you only think it instead of saying it.

5   We are what we are and will never be any different but we can capitalize our good qualities and try to control what is objectionable.

6   Some folks have the instinct of a goose. They lay eggs of fear and then try very hard to hatch them.

7   By all means—read everything that I wrote and then judge me for all that I am or am not.

8   A beach is a place where you can grit your teeth without being mad at anyone.

9   An epigram is an invisible framework of thought made recognizable by shaping it to fit some known experience.

1 Why should a man or a nation feel superior to others when as a matter of fact it was the basic law of environment coupled with time, place and circumstances that made them what they are?

2 It is easier to live with your own faults than it is to live with the other fellow's.

3 Do you men wonder who invented the collar and tie? A woman of course. Who else but a woman would think of a way to collar and tie a man?

4 Human behavior is as unpredictable as a poker hand honestly dealt.

5 Fear evolves from blind darkness and dissolves in the light of dawn.

6 Why try to win the race if you are dead sure you'll be dead before you reach your goal?

7 Coins are made round so they will roll easily from one person to another.

8 Credit is like a humming bird in that it can flit away in the flash of a second.

9 Sin!—What is it?—I never was sure.

1 Frightened little minds of men unable to face the realities of life build illusions around it.

2 Folks have been known to do many things for money—even marry it.

3 It is truly wonderful not to know how many dimes, nickels and pennies we possess.

4 A lucky writer can eat his words and get fat on them.

5 I once knew a man who was a powerful giant. I was certain he could have lifted a good sized house off its foundation if he had taken a notion to do so. I admired his strength. He admired my ability with words. I would have exchanged my ability for his strength—he worked for me.

6 All down through the ages, fools have made important discoveries—that they were fools.

7 Hunger cancels sincerely made obligations between men and nations.

8 A dog will lick the hand that whipped it —so will some women.

PART SIXTEEN

1   Life is like a corrugated scrubbing board, being a continuous run of ups and downs.

2   More than one woman learned with sad regret that while trying to eradicate her husband's shortcomings she was losing him to another who loved him as he was.

3   Some things are as useless as a shaving mug is to the bearded woman in the circus.

4   Never let your head guide your feet while your eyes are closed.

5   All muddy roads traveled on have ruts.

1 Folks are not born with intolerance and hate. They catch it from others like small-pox.

2 A conservative mind is incapable of thinking progressively.

3 Regulation outside the sphere of moderation is tyranny.

4 Regret—a feeling that crawls, itches and burns inside your guts until the brain catches on fire.

5 Time flies and so do our dollars.

6 A woman can love a man with animal devotion and yet hate him for his mental superiority.

7 Some women insist that their husbands make all family decisions—not because they think of them as having better judgment or superior intelligence but because in this way, they can blame them for all mistakes.

8 Because of the peculiar working of one's mind, it takes much more courage to face disappointment in the dark of night than in the light of day.

1   Why waste the bullet if your gun sight is not on the game?

2   There are those who somehow can not enjoy the glorious today because they fear the uncertainty of the coming tomorrow.

3   Democracy is a unifying process accomplishing its aim by tearing down the barriers between all races, creeds and colors.

4   There is never an accredited payoff in winning an argument that lost you a friend.

5   Actually you possess nothing if you don't use it or spend it.

6   There is a wide mental chasm between the visual truth and truth that is realistic.

7   If you are convinced the world owes you a living, the world is convinced it never wanted you in the first place.

8   Common sense is so uncommon that only uncommon people have it.

9   Empty heads live empty lives.

10 Don't deny it—you'll always feel tired when your neighbor asks you for a helping hand.

1 Pressure can maim you, crush you or kill you—it can also shove you forward towards your goal.

2 I can't keep from wondering why it is so many folks keep filling their bags of trouble so full they burst the bags at the seams.

3 Some people are allergic to all bad habits except their own.

4 Every barnyard fowl knows it must scratch the surface to find the most delectable grub.

5 One man acquires profit from knowledge —another from compound interest.

6 There are unimportant men who by a chain of circumstances hold important positions who know of no other way than to make you wait unnecessarily to impress you with their importance.

7 If you think your wife has intuition, forget it. If she had intuition, the chances are good that she never would have married you.

1   All of humanity are offspring of illegitimate ancestors because Adam and Eve were never married.

2   My idea of being semi retired is to devote half of my time to clipping coupons and the other half to spending them.

3   Dreams of grandeur can be made realistic only if in dreaming, you lay each building block realistically.

4   You will never break in half if you bend a little.

5   All of us have at one time or another been guilty of trying to save a plant after we negligently let it die from want of water.

6   To me God is symbolic of something of which I know nothing.

7   Yes indeed—she was sure it was love at first sight—that is, immediately after she ran a D & B on him and found out that his father had set up a million dollar trust fund for him.

8   If you will observe, you will notice that folks who think fast move fast.

1 If you fight back you might lose her—if you don't you will be lost to yourself.

2 There is more than one way for a man to prove he really is a man than by the size of his family.

3 Did you ever see a little pip-squeak try to make itself heard?—Sure you did!

4 If you must ride a back, you'll be more comfortable and safer on a four legged jackass than on a two legged one that might balk and kick your teeth out.

5 Some folks downright refuse to suffer in silence—they make enough noise so that everyone nearby will suffer with them.

6 A big cigar always makes a little man feel big.

7 To what degree of effort would you go to attain that for which you are striving?

8 The life element has no particular shape or size. Heredity and environment shapes its size and destiny be it on this earth or elsewhere.

9 A wife is a married woman who kisses her husband only on pay day.

10 Hysteria feeds on fear and destroys cool and level headed reasoning.

1 A little man mentally small always tries to see himself much bigger than the world sees him.

2 In many countries of the world, men beat their wives for nagging—in the U.S.A. men divorce them.

3 Isn't it peculiar how your stomach ulcers can detect nice people when you meet them and not act up.

4 Some folks assuredly have handicaps of one sort or another but there are many more who are certain they have them without actually knowing what they are.

5 Yes, you can have a louse around you that the law protects against injury.

6 So you admit you have an open mind— but what good is it to you if hornets have taken it over and built a nest in it?

7 America will become a better America only when its people become better Americans.

8 By observation I'm convinced that a new dress gives a woman a feeling of newness and polish.

1 A critic criticizes with the greatest of ease that which he understands the least.

2 I once knew a bachelor who ordered a wedding ring for his bride and a tombstone for himself on the same day.

3 Like a particle of coral, all of us contribute a little something of ourselves to the building of a greater tomorrow.

4 You'll never know your limitation until you break your back trying to find out.

5 To my way of thinking, the longest day in the year is the day you are expecting your landlord with a two months past due rent bill hanging over your head.

6 A rich man once asked his humble slave what he would do if he, the master, set him free and left him his wealth. The slave unhesitatingly answered, "My Good Master, I would buy more slaves."

7 If you are afraid to plant your dollars for investment, think of the farmer if he were afraid to plant his seed because of a possible drouth or insect infestation.

8 Mumbo-Jumbo does not moralize a marriage and neither does a wedding ring.

1 Sometimes folks want badly that which they already have but don't recognize it because it is so close to them.

2 Based on mathematics, if the good qualities in a person counter balance the bad, that person is neither good nor bad—only mathematically so of course.

3 The world is full of successful men and women in every walk of life who became successful not because they weighed the risk they were taking but because they saw no risk.

4 You don't necessarily have to kick a fellow's crazy bone to make him react—you can do it with a word if he has an inferiority complex.

5 Enthusiasm is an arch enemy to Monotony.

6 If you want to find the needle in the haystack—advertise for it.

7 Actually, time will last only so long as there is a human left on this earth who will record the last sunset.

8 An executive in the real sense of the word always faces a problem. The other kind runs away from it.

1 Of course — everyone knows that you can't take it with you but it's a keen satisfaction to know you've got it when you'll need it.

2 Why look so surprised at your bubble that burst—every simpleton knows that sooner or later every bubble must burst.

3 Are you one of those folks who always see a tombstone on every undertaking?

4 Human beings as a rule don't bite, but don't think for a moment that your bark can't inoculate a person with a deadly infection.

5 One half of a split personality actually hates the other half because of their opposite ways of life.

6 Knowing the facts will stabilize your thinking.

7 Words that can bite should have all of their teeth drawn before they are uttered.

8 History proves that a political form of government thrives only in an environment best suited to its needs.

1 In precisely the same way that grey clouds make blue waters look grey, so too will a shadowed mind make all the world look overcast and uninteresting.

2 Are you asking me what a millstone weighs?—I wouldn't know until I knew whether it was on your mind or around your neck.

3 A trifling grievance can grow into a monstrous thing if fed with deadly essence of hate.

4 Some folks are like skunks who try to make you fear them because of the big stink they can make.

5 The best way to win out against a firmly established competitor is to do what you are supposed to do—a little better and a little faster.

6 Parents can make their children miserable but their children if they so choose can make their parents more so.

7 You can't make a name for yourself unless you possess the ingredients with which to make it.

8 Folks sometimes drag their feet because the burden in their heart is overly heavy.

1 I am willing to be called a fool by any one who will prove to me he isn't one himself.

2 A business man refusing to spend money on good advertising is like a farmer refusing to spend his money for good seed.

3 A grandstand my dear fellow is not what you think it is—it's trying to make your wife understand that there is only one boss around your house and that you are it.

4 Ultra conservatism will more likely wreck you than ultra liberalism.

5 Uneasy lies the head that has lice or creditors in his hair.

6 In much the same way as in humanity, nature produces more imperfect diamonds by a great majority.

7 Don't tell yourself you were born unlucky—you are lucky indeed. You might have been born a jackass.

8 Usually a legal obligation has a loophole for escape—a moral obligation has none.

9 It is impossible for your face to conceal your disposition.

1 You won't live longer just because you slept your life away.

2 She wept brokenheartedly—not so much because he no longer lived—but because he didn't know how to live while he was alive.

3 No— you two newlyweds! You two were not the first to discover that life can be beautiful.

4 It's the funniest darn thing—my car seems to have become a part of me. It starts groaning and trembling every time I miss a car payment.

5 A mental stumble and fall can injure you more seriously than tripping and falling on your face.

6 If you win her heart you will have to buy her shoes and give up your freedom.

7 To live life fully one must have a goal— without a goal living becomes aimless, drab and futile.

8 A picnic is a gathering place where you are sure of getting a good quota of protein in every bite you eat—ants.

1 No inded, folks! A goody-goody is not a cookie as you might imagine. It's a pin-head who thinks he was born with a halo around his head.

2 Vice is an opportunist cashing in on human degradation and human frailties.

3 If you insist that all marriages are Heaven made—then I insist that all divorces are home made.

4 Yes—Anabelle was truly beautiful and she just loved beautiful things—even her husband looked beautiful in his coffin after he went through bankruptcy and shot himself.

5 The most inconsiderate taskmaster is usually one who does the least.

6 An ideology of any sort is out of step if the rest of the world is not in step with it.

7 To be important is to be realistic in the realization that you are not important at all.

8 Only the rich can afford hindsight—the poor always have an over abundance of it.

1   Time waits for no man—neither does the due date on a note.

2   When badly in need of a bullet for your gun that can save your life or your freedom, who else but a fool would dicker over the cost of that bullet?

3   There are many incapable men and women in every walk of life who insist on being bottle fed—some even insist that you hold the bottle for them to conserve their energy.

4   It depends on what side of the fence you happen to be on but the fact is that the happiest women are those who have adjusted themselves to agreeing with their husbands.

5   We can safeguard our future by living realistically in the present.

6   Good judgment is a by-product of experience gained as a result of trial and error.

7   A wound need not necessarily be physical to be excruciatingly painful.

8   Every argumentative person has a formula for starting an argument—observe closely and you'll recognize it.

1　Selfish and inconsiderate people get along exceedingly well with each other because they expect nothing from each other.

2　She nagged him, scolded and degraded him in the presence of others and he always forgave her—but when she kicked his dog in a fit of anger, he packed his things and left her.

3　Experience is worthless unless you can make it pay dividends applicable to the price paid.

4　Among women, men are judged by the way their wives dress and the car they drive.

5　If you confess the truth to yourself, you will never be called upon to prove it.

6　If you insist your way is the only way, then you better do it yourself.

7　Lazy people always consider bedrest a luxurious pleasure.

8　In the game of life, you are more likely to deal yourself a losing hand because of your own stupidity than the world will because of its greed.

1 Take a good look at the devil following you in your shadow and you'll be surprised how closely he resembles you.

2 Pennygrubbing like the corn on your toe comes from pressure and like it, can become painfully chronic.

3 Emily is an old maid and no man ever touched her—so the neighbors say—but don't you believe them—Emily lives happily in her dreams that instinct spins for her.

4 You may or may not ever discover yourself but if you do it will be the greatest discovery you will ever make.

5 The tax collector has a headache that aspirins can't cure—and I have a headache too—I voted for him.

6 If you are absolutely certain that everyone you know is peculiar in some way except yourself, go to a mental institution and look the inmates over—I am quite certain you will find a counterpart of yourself.

7 Every day carries a high price tag. No one can afford to lose even a minute of it.

1 Life is for the living—the grave is for the dead, so pull yourself out of your lethargy and live while you can.

2 A fool always baits the trap that springs him.

3 Every kiss has an exchange value.

4 Some women are like bees making honey except that one looks for nectar, the other for money.

5 The fellow who can write a check for a million dollars and have it honored needs no pep talk, either from you or from me.

6 I dislike people who smile only at a funeral.

7 Yes indeed! John Smart was the best bookkeeper I ever knew. He only made one mistake. He still has two more years to count depending on good behavior.

8 Home is a place where all of your unpaid bills concentrate.

9 Some folks are just built that way. She was certain the eggs were fresh because the sign said so.

10 Love blooms—and so does a thistle.

1   It is most embarrassing to create a lie and then be forced to face it face to face.

2   It's a good thing we are living in a topsy-turvy world, otherwise no one would want to leave it and the world would get overcrowded.

3   A bed fully paid for is much more restful than one yet to be paid for.

4   She married him because she was weak and he was strong—first she monopolized him and then she possessed him and so hid her weakness in his strength by tactful maneuvering.

5   What I have observed and written regarding human nature in this generation will be applicable to human nature ten thousand generations hence.

6   You are not your own master if a whip is crackling behind you.

7   There are other ways of going to hell than by grabbing a devil's tail and hanging on.

8   Respecting other people's opinions will dignify your own.

1 If you search high and you search low, you will never find any visible realistic purpose in the creation of all that is.

2 He loved her for her money and he loved her for her youth—he dissipated her money and she dissipated her youth.

3 If you don't like the way your boss runs his business buy him out and show him how his business should have been run.

4 You are lost to yourself, your family and the world when you become resigned to thinking that what must be will be.

5 Why be angry at the world? Remember that the world is putting up with you and your idiosyncrasies with considerable patience.

6 Self-centered happiness is always short-lived.

7 She was a habitual nag and scolded at every opportunity. After a few years of listening to her, her voice sounded to him like his neighbor's dog barking angrily.

8 Hate justifies every diabolical act regardless of reason.

1 Eccentricities become indelible and impossible to eradicate after fifty.

2 A contribution is purchase money not charity if the donor receives any satisfaction in donating it.

3 The only time a woman can drive a man is when she has a firm grip on his heartstrings.

4 A tyrant can always justify his actions by interpreting his own definition of justice.

5 If your wife would be honest with you she would admit that she would rather have buttered bread when she is hungry than your buttered kisses.

6 Ugly tempered people should find ugly tempered mates and so give each other a ready outlet for their ugly dispositions.

7 You can't heal a broken spirit by encasing it in a cast.

8 The price of a quarrel runs painfully high and can never be had at a bargain price.

9 A real scientist no longer believes in the word "impossible." To him his project is only seemingly impossible.

1 A plow horse outlives a race horse because the plow horse instinctively takes hard work in a slow and steady pace.

2 Placing your confidence in a person will take you off guard against that person.

3 There are those who just love to cackle over their grudges like a brooding hen cackling over her nest of eggs.

4 Some women get intoxicated on flattery quicker than on whiskey—and carry a longer hang-over.

5 Bygone youth can be appreciated best at a distance of fifty years or more.

6 When you are entirely pleased with yourself and can see no fault you are without a doubt head-over-heels in love with yourself.

7 Be sensible and don't think for a moment that environment adjusted itself to human needs—Man definitely adjusted himself to his environment.

8 Frustration and self-pity are inseparable. Where you find one you are certain to find the other.

1 Marriage is like a grapefruit—you've got to squeeze the good out of it.

2 Fussy little minds are always in a dither and never miss a chance to make a big stink over nothing.

3 Sometimes a fool can find what you have been trying to find and couldn't.

4 Every high riding ego must burst before it can come down to earth.

5 To strive for an important goal and reach it, a man must be inspired and feel that he is important to someone who is important to him.

6 In a proposal, instinct inoculates you with desire and puts the words on your tongue.

7 Mediocrity creates nothing that is more than mediocre—only innate emotion and ability can create a masterpiece.

8 If you are waiting for a job to come your way that will pay you what you think you are worth, you are as a matter of fact worth nothing.

9 Any so-called thing of beauty to be appreciated must be in its right environment.

1   The first man to reach the moon could make a fortune by canning moonbeams and selling them to young lovers.

2   Abstaining is not a sign of moral strength. On the contrary—it's a sign of weakness because the abstainer fears testing his sense of self-control.

3   Teaching a child the 3 R's is less important to his well-being than teaching him to co-ordinate his thinking with right living in association with others not like himself.

4   Never skate over thin ice unless you have the utmost confidence in your speed and are certain you can maintain it.

5   You acquire the knack for doing things by doing them.

6   It's a good thing to stub your toe every now and then because it keeps you alert to the ruts at your feet.

7   Promoters are the backbone of industry and create the seed pods of production and progress.

8   Couples too often drift far apart never getting closer together than their beds.

1   To be free of desire is to be free of need.

2   Some folks just love half-baked truths eaten with honey and garnished with lies.

3   Clean hands will immunize you against blackmail.

4   One side of a split personality never for a moment trusts the other side.

5   Every woman has a correlated affinity for some man and no woman so correlated can resist that man.

6   Politeness like a steam shovel can make a deep impression.

7   To condemn a human being to death does not solve the problem whatever it may be—it is legalized murder and nothing else.

8   When you are itching for an argument—bite yourself—you'll find it a sure cure for the urge.

9   By observation I am convinced that marriage is sometimes like a shoe that pinches —you can bear it if you like the shoe well enough.

10 Misconstruing a friend's intent can be fatal to your friendship.

1 A mad dog department executive can inoculate with madness all who are subordinate to him.

2 Hope anesthetizes fear and withdraws its stinger.

3 Your mind can make your burden twice the burden that it is or lessen it by half.

4 Some folks if they really got acquainted with themselves would hate themselves.

5 A classic is like moldy cheese. Not everyone likes it but those who do relish it for its moldy flavor.

6 Journalism at its so-called best is an exposure of private lives highlighted to public view and review.

7 Nature makes demands without compromise on all things within its domain.

8 A fluent writer can create words with eyes, ears and power of speech. Such a writer can live luxuriously by his pen.

9 The law of evolution is governed by pattern and timing designed and dictated by environment. Identical conditions millions of light years distant will produce identical histories of creation.

1   You can wear out your best friend's welcome mat by muddying it too often.

2   What you put away today you'll find some other day—around your middle.

3   In a man's world a woman's only defense lies in her sex, her tongue and her tears.

4   An empty cup is like an empty life—nothing put in, nothing to take out.

5   It is impossible for you to elevate yourself by lowering the level of the other fellow.

6   Life is incidental in the scheme of evolution—there is nothing to indicate any importance for it.

7   The worst thing about success is that it keeps you wondering—wondering how you got there and wondering how long you'll stay there.

8   Imagination undermines judgment and buries it deep under.

9   It's a good trait of character to forgive and forget and good sense to remember that you did it.

1 There are many who would have continued their education but did not because they were convinced that they were born smart and did not need to further it.

2 Money madness callouses the conscience and blinds the eyes of Justice.

3 There is a breaking point in the strongest cable ever produced by man as there is also a breaking point in every human mind.

4 Opposition invariably sets up a barrier against good sense and reason.

5 Very few fathers ever admitted a bad trait of character in his son having been inherited from him.

6 There is significance in the fact that no fruit is palatable for human consumption until the seed or seeds within are ripe and ready for next season's planting.

7 The thing you over-reach for can crush you.

8 If you were once in the driver's seat you will resist consciously or otherwise every effort by anyone attempting to drive you.

1 The pig that squeals the loudest has the biggest bellyache.

2 By all means, trust wholeheartedly the God of your choice but keep a steady finger on the trigger and a keen eye on the gun sight.

3 He initialed the tree deeply with her initial entwined in his. In the course of years the tree healed its wound but his wound never healed.

4 Friendships like the soles of your shoes wear out and need replacement from time to time.

5 If you are money-mad no amount you ever acquire will ever satisfy your craving for it.

6 A warm personality can thaw out a frozen face.

7 When you live in a community you are under moral obligation to that community to keep your dogs off the lawns, your skunk out of their beds and your owl out of their hair.

8 Fanaticism is a conditioning of the mind that blockades reality.

1   More likely than not if you try to convince your friends to bury the hatchets they are using on each other they will turn on you and chop you down.

2   You can lose your appetite for anything by getting bilious from it.

3   An old head will never rid itself of old impressions.

4   Opportunity as it passes you by never has the courtesy of even saying, "Hi."

5   Discontentment is a merciless driver with a cat-o'-nine-tails driving its victims blindly from place to place.

6   Freedom is like a great big plump olive. It can be appreciated only by those who have a taste for it.

7   With enough sweating you can pull yourself out of the rut that mired you.

8   All that a cow gets out of life is the pleasure of chewing her cud. How many people get more?

9   Every man is a pawn in the hands of the tax collector.

10   Referring to our friends and neighbors—peace is like a jar of preserves—it takes sugar to preserve it.

1 Every marriage is a trial marriage until death or divorce do them part.

2 The mind's eye under duress always sees Calamity pregnant with an expectant litter of little calamities.

3 Close association can kindle an all consuming love affair and create barriers impossible to surmount.

4 Occasionally we are forced by circumstances to deal with people who are so viciously rabid that even mad dogs are afraid to cross their path.

5 To be successful, a marriage must be pleasantly intoxicating or it goes flat like spoiled wine.

6 There is dignity in every job well done.

7 Too often when a man can't support himself he marries a woman with money so she can be his crutch.

8 Death is feared most by those who haven't lived yet.

9 Be realistic—it will do you no good to cry for the dream that escaped you.

1 Most neighbors because they say, "Good morning," to you think it entitles them to the privilege of letting their dogs mess up your lawn and ruin your flower beds.

2 The mind can only digest the ingredients of thought that are prepared for it.

3 Forcing your daughter to marry a man against her will is like switching your cow to the bull pen.

4 Perpetual motion economy started when a genius in Washington decided it is just as easy to print government bonds as it is paper money with less disturbance to the economy of the world—buy bonds.

5 The same day you get home from your honeymoon you will know who is going to be at the head of your household.

6 A dark skin is superficial and differs in shade but the color of the blood in all of humanity is pretty much the same.

7 To be wrong is not to be right of course but what is wrong in this generation can be right in the next—so what is being wrong?

1 When a man tries to be congenial with his wife, his wife if she holds the purse strings never gives up her vigilance and suspicion of his intent.

2 All of humanity will have disappeared from the face of the earth before evolution will have had time to evolve the first perfect man.

3 What's in a name anyhow? I once knew a man whose name was I. M. Rich but who was actually a hobo begging for handouts.

4 Sleep is not a thing you can turn off and on like a light switch when in reality the mind is the switch.

5 Undetected worms in a business or in a ship's hull can cause them both to flounder and sink.

6 You'll never go wrong if your conscience will always know what your hands are doing and where your feet are taking you —provided of course that you have a conscience.

7 A man belittles himself when he belittles others whom he thinks are inferior to himself.

1 Our dollars are like greased cart wheels —they keep silently and rapidly rolling along until they are out of sight.

2 Most people are built that way. They feel painfully insignificant when their bank balance shrinks to insignificance.

3 Woe unto the man who holds authority tightly gripped in his right hand and doesn't know what his subordinate left hand is doing.

4 The man who inherits a million dollars does not inherit the ulcers it took to make the million—he will invariably cultivate and grow his own.

5 A dictionary has all the makings of the best novel ever written—but it lacks life and experience which must come from the author.

6 Man contains within himself many pent-up characteristics and moods—drunkenness brings them forth and exposes them to full view.

7 A fool looked into a mirror and observed himself closely. "Sure enough," he mumbled, "everybody I know looks a little like me."

1   To what degree a person can irritate you depends on your degree of liking or disliking that person.

2   South Australian natives use the hollow skull of a former enemy as a drinking cup—an ingenious way indeed to satisfy the thirst for revenge.

3   When a man and wife find themselves unsuited for each other they can be certain that in the next fifty years of married life and strife all adjustments to each other will have been made. Living together thereafter will be in perfect harmony—except maybe agreeing where they are to be buried.

4   An unsuspected person who dislikes you intensely in the guise of a friend can be fatal to your happiness and well-being.

5   Saccharin is something a widow uses in big doses to talk a doddering widower into marriage.

6   A man needs an unwavering iron will to protect him against women and on the other hand women need their sex appeal to break down his unwavering will.

1 Our mind catches the fleeting years and stores them in the archives of our memory for future reference.

2 You can preserve your friendships by giving your friends the money they want to borrow from you instead of loaning it to them and never getting it back.

3 The word "economize" loses its meaning after you spend your last dollar.

4 A belief that is not realistically acceptable to your mind should never be forced upon it—to do otherwise is to make yourself believe in what you know is a lie.

5 Desire stimulates and feeds inspiration until desire cools off.

6 After fifty the accumulation of years gains weight and when all of them climb on your back to roost like a flock of vultures your knees will buckle under you.

7 If you must brag—brag about your todays not your yesterdays because your yesterdays are dead and buried in the eternal past.

1   If we could declare a national edict to make no mistakes for one year and made none, we could pay off our national debt with what we saved.

2   To make a high record jump or make a million one needs room to build up momentum.

3   Taxes are like yeast in dough—we just naturally expect them to rise.

4   Time seems to pass more quickly while working piecework than it does working by the hour.

5   A big woman with a big heart can not give forth greater love than a little woman half her weight.

6   Stupid men do stupid things and for some unknown reason smart ones follow in their footsteps.

7   Life for all intent and purpose ends when productivity ends—giving a helping hand with a smile to one who needs it extends one's productivity.

8   The flying wings of time can fly in one direction only and has no way of turning back.

1 Civilization is still in its metamorphic state like a larvae passing through its pupa transformaton.

2 Familiarity nowadays seldom breeds contempt but familiarity can result in breeding a family.

3 Living life is not experience gained if one remembers nothing or learned nothing as a result of living.

4 The right to vote is the most valuable asset that any nation can possess. Without it a nation soon becomes the pawn of tyrants.

5 Man found a way to fly over mountains when he came to the conclusion it took too long to climb or burrow under them.

6 The elements of luck are made up of a combination of time, place and circumstances. Intelligence is no part of it.

7 You can't fence in your wee bit of heaven because it has no defined boundaries.

8 Fear of old age without having financial security brings on a devastating madness that nothing but security can cure.

1 It is every person's right to believe only that which his mind can conceive and will accept.

2 Historians will record this generation as the era of unions. We don't know yet whether the unions will take over and run our government or our government take over and run the unions.

3 It is impossible to combine fire with water without a steaming eruption.

4 If deformity of a sort was universal, we as we are would be the deformed ones.

5 A little girl's imagination can make her see her doll as she wants to see it— parents can also make themselves see their children in a like manner.

6 Antagonism and Prejudice have been inseparable buddies since infancy. They grew up on the same kind of milk and now go hunting together for the same kind of game.

7 To doubt what is supposed to be an established fact proves conclusively that you have a mind of your own.

1 You can discover a nation's shortcomings by its laws.

2 A dullard can never cultivate a taste for epigrams because he lacks the sense of analysis.

3 Human discards—every city in the world has droves of them as witness Skid Row in your city. Don't smile, my friend—it just so happens that some people skid easier than others.

4 The voice of hunger is the voice of Desperation and is capable of murder.

5 The brain is an electronic device in control of our impulses. When it will be as well understood as television, all penal institutions will be turned into hospitals for intellect repairs and correction—and man will then truly have become the master of his own destiny.

6 Not a thing on earth can be beautiful to you if it does not excite your senses.

7 The law of probability based on chance makes it likely that the earth will some day collide with a star.

1   Based on biological fact our chance of having been born as we are was one chance in one hundred trillion. With these facts provable mathematically— be yourself and don't attach any importance to your status of birth.

2   It is a waste of money to bedeck your wife with diamonds if your wife's friends don't know the difference between a real diamond and a zircon.

3   The other fellow's opinion is often difficult to swallow and will stick in your throat because it isn't sugar-coated and flavored to your taste.

4   Without spadework you will never know what lies under the rock pile of your curiosity.

5   You can measure the degree of your patience by the boiling point of your impatience.

6   You can be certain of staying out of jail for assault and battery by letting your self-control lead your fighting impulse on a leash.

7   Wheels that stand still get nowhere.

1   Idiosyncrasies are made of a cement-like substance that once formed and set—never changes.

2   Most heirs never hold onto their inheritance because they had never learned how to prevent it from dissolving.

3   Any man's achievement is never more than a link in a long chain of achievements that preceded him.

4   Girls—don't give up hope if you are over thirty—most men believe that by thirty a girl has had time to save up some money.

5   Yesterday's spent moments are like yesterday's spent pennies—we can never hope to retrieve them.

6   Individual love selection is inherent and originates from a magnetic impulse created by two individuals with a sexual affinity for each other.

7   If you lay an egg of fear your mind will incubate and mother it.

8   A companionate marriage might possibly turn out to be a successful marriage if the woman never aged.

1   Every great man in every walk of life living or dead could never have become great if circumstances of time and place had not occurred exactly right for him.

2   Lack of consideration for the other fellow's things shows lack of character in one's make up.

3   The joke that you think is so funny if spoken can strike a human target and produce a wound that will infect.

4   It is possible to run so fast for shelter that you would run into an obstruction and dash out your brains.

5   Some men are like the carpenter who sharpened his tools but wouldn't go to work because he didn't want to dull his tools again.

6   A petty mind creates petty reasons to squabble.

7   Some people lack the homing instinct and must always be on the move to be content.

8   Sometimes a man must fight desperately with himself to get the best of himself.

CONCLUSION

I tasted the fruit from the tree of life and found it bittersweet yet delightful—but the season ended all too soon. Cold winter set in white with snow. The branches once heavily laden with fruit that delighted my senses are now bare and gnarled and all that was is but a nostalgic memory.

INDEX OF CONTENTS

Classified Words of Subject Matter
First figure is page number; second figure is epigram
referred to.

137, 3; 149, 8
Advertising 241, 2
Advice 101, 7;
116, 7; 120, 5; 165, 6
Affair 24, 3; 260, 3
Affection 58, 3; 211, 9
Affectionate 120, 3
Affiliations 198, 1
Affinity 119, 5;
254, 5; 271, 6
Affliction 74, 6
Afraid 89, 4; 127, 7;
169, 1; 237, 7; 260, 4
Africa 101, 6
Age 30, 2; 39, 7; 44, 2;
48, 1; 73, 1; 74, 10; 84, 6;
87, 5; 90, 7; 92, 1;
126, 6; 167, 2; 179, 3;
197, 2; 198, 8; 244, 2
Aged 271, 8
Ages 23, 6; 78, 1
Agent 186, 5
Aging 101, 1; 189, 3;
242, 7
Agony 185, 2
Agree 58, 7
Aim 44, 3; 232, 3
Aimless 242, 7
Air 108, 7; 112, 6; 131, 4;
181, 3; 203, 4
Alarm 183, 8
Alarming 183, 8
Alcohol 96, 8
Alcoholic 28, 3
Alert 253, 6
Alibi 54, 9; 61, 2;
164, 4; 193, 2
Alimony 46, 1; 111, 6;
127, 3
All consuming 260, 3
Alone 53, 3; 58, 4;
73, 9; 94, 5; 119, 1
Alter 44, 11; 108, 6
Alternative 201, 8
Ambition 8, 3; 44, 3;
55, 9; 58, 1; 86, 4;

111, 7; 133, 2; 145, 3;
169, 4; 170, 2; 184, 7;
190, 4; 219, 9
America 236, 7
American 79, 9
Americans 43, 6; 99, 1;
236, 7
Amusement 46, 4
Ancestor 118, 3
Ancestors 192, 1; 208, 1;
234, 1
Ancestry 6, 8
Ancient 86, 8; 146, 5;
187, 7
Anger 9, 4; 15, 3;
22, 1; 22, 5; 37, 8;
115, 8; 157, 8; 245, 2
Animation 161, 5;
208, 5
Answer 60, 1; 63, 2;
93, 2; 102, 2; 152, 5;
191, 8; 221, 7
Ant 38, 3
Antagonism 268, 6
Antique 115, 7
Antiques 73, 4; 85, 4
Antiquity 115, 7;
213, 2; 218, 7
Annual 231, 7
Anticipate 212, 8
Anxiety 135, 1
Anxious 203, 6
Anyone 33, 1; 43, 4;
46, 2; 65, 5; 101, 7;
102, 4; 111, 8; 125, 8;
136, 5; 168, 4; 168, 6
Anything 42, 6; 63, 3;
64, 3; 76, 4; 83, 9;
127, 5; 129, 6; 170, 6;
178, 5
Apologize 3, 3;
122, 1
Appeal 264, 6
Appearance 137, 8;
186, 2
Appetite 33, 8; 77, 4;

115, 5; 141, 3; 259, 2
Applaud 93, 7
Applicable 245, 3
Appointment 151, 2
Appreciate 54, 5;
204, 7
Appreciation 81, 4; 129, 1;
129, 2; 167, 2
Architect 79, 5
Archives 113, 2; 265, 1
Argue 142, 1
Argument 44, 7; 142, 1;
215, 5; 222, 5; 232, 4;
244, 8; 254, 8
Arm 74, 3
Army 30, 2; 68, 3
Arouse 104, 7
Art 42, 1; 83, 4;
147, 5; 155, 5
Artist 5, 3; 204, 7
Artists 83, 4
Assault 270, 7
Assembly 164, 8
Asset 35, 2; 67, 5;
75, 2; 172, 2; 187, 2;
267, 4
Assets 116, 8
Associates 44, 2;
138, 8
Association 253, 3; 260, 3
Assumption 40, 4
Astigmatism 77, 6
Asylum 225, 5
Atheist 56, 7
Atheists 131, 2
Atmosphere 197, 3
Attack 223, 7
Attain 235, 7
Attainable 82, 5
Attained 174, 8
Attainment 32, 7;
34, 5; 55, 9
Attic 67, 4
Attics 177, 8
Attract 51, 9;
117, 2; 122, 6

Attribute 68, 4
Attributes 44, 8; 54, 5;
182, 2
Audience 90, 1; 93, 7
Authenticity 117, 5
Author 145, 9;
178, 7; 263, 5
Authority 63, 6; 210, 2;
263, 3
Automobile 214, 8
Automobiles 43, 6
Autumn 68, 8
Avalanche 140, 5
Avarice 153, 4
Awakening 74, 9
Awfulness 155, 5
Axe 165, 4
Axes 142, 3; 193, 9

B

Babe 120, 7
Babies 27, 6
Baby 33, 7; 56, 2;
147, 2
Bachelor 32, 3; 66, 8;
72, 6; 159, 1; 214, 1;
237, 2
Backbone 61, 7;
96, 9; 253, 7
Backward 212, 4
Bad 90, 1
Bag 123, 2; 145, 7;
152, 2
Bags 161, 7
Balance 171, 8;
238, 2; 263, 2
Ball, 199, 6
Balloon 135, 7
Band 124, 9
Bank 52, 2; 67, 5;
74, 8; 171, 8; 176, 9;
191, 1; 263, 2
Banker 24, 5

Boot 127, 3
Bore 97, 4
Bores 174, 9; 200, 3;
208, 4
Born 31, 5; 38, 6;
53, 4; 69, 4; 84, 6;
102, 8; 119, 1; 119, 5;
135, 6; 153, 8; 157, 1;
162, 7; 165, 5; 195, 4;
197, 6; 198, 4; 200, 6;
225, 4; 225, 9; 231, 1;
241, 7; 243, 2; 257, 1
Borrow 37, 6; 67, 5;
95, 10; 99, 3; 191, 1;
265, 2
Borrowed 134, 3; 227, 1
Boss 68, 9; 89, 4;
212, 2; 241 3; 249, 3
Bottle 29, 3; 38, 1;
168, 9; 199, 7; 219, 4;
244, 3
Bottom 91, 6; 204, 6;
208, 8
Bottomless 77, 4; 102, 1
Boulders 140, 5
Bound 163, 7; 169, 4;
211, 8; 218, 4
Boundaries 83, 7; 267, 7
Boundary 11, 1
Bow 67, 4
Bowlegged 128, 6
Bowls 86, 5
Boy 34, 3; 52, 1; 114, 6;
117, 8; 129, 7; 203, 5;
203, 8; 226, 4
Boyhood 142, 2
Boys 125, 2; 129, 7
Brace 132, 7
Brag 6, 8; 31, 1;
33, 9; 121, 2; 185, 1;
265, 7
Brain 42, 9; 47, 4; 67, 6;
83, 3; 155, 7; 161, 2;
169, 7; 174, 9; 208, 4;
231, 5; 269, 5
Brains 131, 4; 272, 4

Brakes 49, 8
Brave 43, 3; 80, 3;
129, 9
Bravery 43, 3
Breach 46, 1; 108, 6
Bread 39, 5; 106, 2;
191, 3; 250, 5
Breakfast 139, 2; 219, 5
Breast 22, 3
Breath 160, 7;
192, 3; 205, 6; 209, 3
Breathed 112, 6
Breathing 108, 7
Breed 168, 2
Brevity 99, 8
Brick 20, 5; 80, 3;
146, 2; 164, 8
Bride 133, 5; 237, 2
Bridges 162, 2
Bright 51, 9; 176, 3;
176, 7
Brightest 171, 7
Brilliance 71, 8; 128, 1; 205, 7
Brilliant 53, 9; 197, 5
Brimstone 77, 2
Broaden 75, 4
Broad-minded 27, 7
Broken 53, 6; 85, 10;
250, 7
Brokenheartedly 242, 2
Brooding 41, 1; 93, 2
Broom 57, 1
Brother 139, 3; 193, 2;
203, 3; 225, 6
Brothers 86, 8; 214, 1
Brow 58, 1
Browbeat 49, 6
Brush 158, 1
Brutality 123, 6
Bubble 30, 7; 239, 2
Bubbles 192, 3
Buckle 265, 6
Bucks 101, 8; 223, 4
Bud 58, 1
Buddies 268, 6
Budding 179, 3; 192, 2

Candy coated 27, 2
Cannibal 118, 1;
219, 2
Capable 131, 1; 175, 5;
182, 8; 199, 8; 208, 5;
212, 5; 269, 4
Capacity 71, 4
Capital 163, 1
Capitalism 161, 4
Captivity 128, 3
Car 80, 6; 160, 2;
242, 4; 245, 4
Cards 165, 8; 174, 6
Care 74, 1; 105, 4;
193, 3
Career 181, 2
Carpenter 272, 5
Carrier 148, 8
Cars 208, 10
Cart 263, 1
Cartridge 169, 2
Case 11, 5; 192, 7
Cash 199, 3
Casket 208, 6
Castle 62, 7
Castles 48, 1; 210, 4
Cat 84, 3; 85, 1;
124, 7; 125, 1; 141, 8;
152, 2; 201, 3
Catalog 94, 5
Caterers 198, 2
Cat-o'-nine-tails 259, 5
Cause 71, 1; 196, 1
Caution 69, 1; 72, 6;
108, 2; 124, 8; 193, 5
Cautious 193, 1
Cave 86, 8
Celebrants 193, 10
Cell 110, 5
Cells 151, 4
Cent 146, 1
Centenarian 197, 2
Centuries 199, 5
Ceremony 63, 6
Cesspools 20, 2
Chain 14, 2; 18, 9;

41, 9; 148, 8; 161, 6;
163, 7; 192, 1; 199, 6;
200, 5; 218, 4; 233, 6;
271, 3
Chair 94, 4; 133, 4
Challenge 8, 2; 49, 4;
209, 3
Champion 214, 9
Chance 22, 2; 84, 9;
103, 4; 131, 3; 137, 7;
196, 2; 225, 3; 226, 9;
252, 2; 269, 7; 270, 1
Chances 88, 8;
106, 5; 108, 3; 108, 8;
116, 9; 119, 4; 186, 8;
233, 7
Change 19, 5; 37, 5;
73, 1; 81, 6; 99, 4;
127, 9; 154, 7; 163, 2;
186, 2; 188, 1; 256, 9;
257, 5; 272, 2
Character 112, 4
Characteristics 189, 3;
210, 3; 263, 6
Characters 207, 3
Charity 58, 3; 77, 3;
107, 5; 116, 9; 118, 4;
250, 2
Charm 14, 4; 33, 8; 54, 3;
134, 9; 163, 6
Chart 18, 4
Chase 85, 7; 91, 1;
129, 4; 145, 6
Chasm 232, 6
Cheap 223, 4
Cheated 180, 2
Cheating 180, 2
Check 29, 8; 80, 6;
125, 2; 247, 5
Cheeks 43, 6
Cheer 196, 7
Cheese 37, 9; 128, 2;
153, 9; 255, 5
Chemical 215, 6; 208, 8
Chess 29, 5
Chestnut 186, 2

152, 3
Creatures 218, 7
Credit 4, 4; 24, 5;
24, 6; 71, 5; 89, 4;
107, 7; 124, 9; 171, 8;
174, 2; 225, 7; 227, 1;
228, 8
Creditor 16, 3; 19, 8;
27, 2; 68, 3; 123, 3;
216, 8
Creditors 55, 8; 113, 3;
241, 5
Creed 51, 8; 106, 9
Creeds 232, 3
Crest 169, 6
Crime 11, 5; 43, 4;
78, 1; 118, 5; 180, 9;
196, 1; 217, 8
Crimes 57, 7; 85, 6
Criminal 45, 4; 208, 9
Critic 207, 2; 237, 1
Criticism 112, 1; 113, 1;
207, 2
Crooked 193, 6
Crop 201, 5; 223, 1
Cross 165, 6; 260, 4
Crossroads 136, 3
Crow 81, 7
Crowd 43, 2; 256, 10
Crown 36, 5
Cruel 55, 3; 109, 8;
195, 6
Crush 233, 2; 257, 7
Crushes 136, 1; 148, 8
Crushing 36, 9; 132, 7;
182, 8; 208, 5; 216, 9
Crust 169, 5
Crutch 260, 7
Crutches 111, 5; 174, 2;
176, 8; 201, 1
Cry 97, 8; 260, 9
Cud 259, 8
Cultivate 171, 2;
181, 6; 263, 4; 269, 2
Cunning 99, 4
Cup 144, 5; 256, 4;

264, 2
Cur 175, 3
Curb 160, 2
Cure 70, 8; 136, 9;
168, 9; 196, 1;
199, 7; 246, 5; 254, 8;
267, 8
Curiosity 146, 7; 270, 5
Curious 23, 4
Curse 20, 3; 218, 2
Curtain 62, 6
Custom 106, 4
Cut 60, 5; 66, 2;
67, 7; 119, 7; 122, 7;
127, 3; 149, 6; 222, 10
Cuts 145, 2
Cutting 143, 9;
163, 8; 175, 5
Cycle 8, 5; 209, 8
Cyclone 34, 4; 92, 4

D

Dad 44, 2
Dagger 48, 5; 99, 8
Dame Fortune 224, 7
Damper 108, 7
Dance 186, 1
Dancing 36, 7; 84, 3
Danger 49, 8; 108, 2;
204, 5; 211, 9
Dangerous 33, 4; 86, 3;
91, 8; 125, 9; 145, 8
Dangle 130, 7
Dare 110, 2
Dark 27, 8; 78, 1;
119, 5; 129, 6; 155, 4;
213, 9
Darkening 163, 2; 180, 8
Darkness 8, 6; 43, 1;
112, 7; 164, 2; 228, 5
Date 34, 3
Daughter 161, 9;
261, 3
Daughters 149, 4

195, 7
Discard 101, 2
Discards 269, 3
Discontentment 44, 6; 259, 5
Discount 99, 7
Discourtesy 124, 2
Discover 20, 1; 23, 2;
32, 6; 62, 6; 64, 6;
76, 6; 84, 2; 132, 5;
138, 8; 159, 6; 242, 3;
246, 4; 269, 1
Discovered 91, 5; 142, 3
Discoveries 229, 8
Discovery 246, 4
Discredits 179, 6
Discrimination 132, 3;
196, 3
Disease 90, 9; 171, 4;
204, 1
Disgrace 188, 6
Disguise 35, 7; 67, 2;
128, 5
Disgusting 106, 6
Dish 54, 6
Dishonest 38, 5; 49, 1;
85, 7
Dishonesty 193, 6
Disillusionment 143, 7
Dislike 122, 1; 214, 6;
247, 6
Dislikes 136, 5; 155, 2;
186, 6
Dismal 23, 1
Disobedience 190, 1
Disparaging 47, 7
Display 60, 8; 66, 8;
82, 4; 95, 3; 138, 6;
153, 8; 192, 7; 198, 5
Disposition 16, 8; 50, 8;
69, 4; 71, 1; 189, 2;
220, 7; 241, 9
Dispositions 250, 6
Dissension 149, 6;
184, 7; 218, 8
Dissipated 62, 1; 249, 2
Dissolve 43, 1

Distance 60, 2; 87, 6; 197, 7;
211, 6; 251, 5
Distasteful 113, 9
Distinction 214, 4
Distort 77, 6
Distorted 142, 4
Distract 154, 4
Distress 12, 4
Distrust 149, 1; 218, 8
Disturbance 261, 4
Disturbing 27, 2; 157, 3
Dive 53, 7; 83, 9
Dividends 96, 4; 97, 5;
245, 3
Division 187, 7
Divorce 43, 7; 120, 9;
161, 3; 184, 7; 236, 2;
260, 1
Divorces 72, 1 243, 4
Doctor 196, 7
Doddering 264, 5
Dog 24, 3; 24, 6;
32, 5; 49, 6; 65, 4;
125, 3; 127, 7; 129, 5;
138, 3; 143, 4; 145, 6;
161, 6; 177, 8; 179, 2;
186, 3; 187, 3; 201, 3;
205, 1; 214, 2; 220, 7; 223, 7;
226, 7; 229, 8; 245, 2; 255, 1
Dogmas 157, 1
Dogs 129, 5; 135, 3;
159, 5; 168, 2; 258, 8;
260, 4; 261, 1
Doings 117, 7
Doll 64, 6; 268, 5
Dollar 5, 8; 51, 9;
60, 8; 107, 2; 121, 2;
130, 4; 141, 5; 181, 1;
265, 3
Dollars 33, 7; 51, 2;
55, 7; 70, 4; 79, 3;
101, 5; 231, 6; 237, 7;
247, 5; 263, 1; 263, 4
Domain 255, 7
Dominate 71, 9
Donkey 90, 4; 111, 8

Door 47, 8; 48, 4; 90, 4;
90, 8; 110, 5; 115, 5;
127, 2; 143, 4; 144, 1;
150, 3; 150, 4; 183, 10;
184, 10; 206, 8
Dose 113, 1
Doses 264, 5
Double 106, 7; 157, 5
Double-faced 26, 6
Doubt 8, 6; 10, 7; 21, 9;
25, 3; 87, 1; 268, 7
Doubtful 173, 7
Douse 30, 7; 79, 6
Down 67, 7; 76, 6;
80, 1; 91, 4; 94, 6;
106, 7; 107, 3; 123, 5;
126, 1; 132, 7; 135, 9;
140, 5; 144, 3; 160, 6;
162, 2; 174, 7; 185, 10;
193, 9; 195, 5
Downtrodden 11, 3
Drab 51, 6; 242, 7
Drag 210, 3; 240, 8
Drastic 110, 8
Draw 143, 9;
154, 3; 157, 7; 244, 3
Dread 98, 3
Dream 9, 7; 260, 9
Dreaming 66, 3;
234, 3
Dreams 24, 4; 42, 8;
46, 6; 62, 7; 103, 2;
119, 7; 210, 4; 234, 3;
246, 3
Dreamy-eyed 120, 7
Dreary 135, 9
Dress 110, 8; 116, 1;
236, 8; 245, 4
Dresses 94, 5
Drift 25, 5; 253, 8
Drill 42, 9; 174, 9;
208, 4
Drink 58, 4
Drinks 58, 4
Drip 17, 2
Drippings 21, 1

Drive 49, 8;
150, 6; 245, 4; 250, 3;
257, 8
Driver 153, 9; 259, 5
Drivers 73, 9
Drives 43, 7; 73, 5
Driving 44, 6; 122, 3;
145, 3
Drone 100, 3
Drop 76, 6; 82, 3
Drops 159, 2
Dross 78, 7
Drouth 124, 5; 148, 1;
237, 7
Drown 78, 5; 124, 7;
173, 7; 217, 3
Drowning 30, 5; 106, 9
Drum 60, 7
Drunk 29, 3; 98, 3
Drunkard 30, 3
Duck 80, 3
Dull 73, 2; 139, 6;
272, 5
Dullard 269, 2
Dumb 106, 5
Dump 47, 6; 123, 7
Dumps 47, 6
Duress 260, 2
Dust 86, 8; 115, 7;
142, 6; 189, 6; 200, 9;
218, 7
Duty 157, 5; 163, 7;
211, 8
Dynamic 122, 3
Dynamite 206, 1
Dynasties 217, 5

E

Eagle 195, 5
Ear 17, 3; 46, 2;
208, 2
Earn 99, 3
Ears 30, 6; 93, 6;
131, 4; 182, 3; 199, 8

114, 8; 126, 2; 145, 8;
156, 3; 170, 8; 177, 7;
191, 4; 199, 8; 204, 8;
206, 2; 207, 6; 213, 4;
216, 3; 219, 1; 230, 4;
255, 8; 257, 2

F

Face 19, 5; 27, 8;
29, 1; 33, 4; 36, 3; 37, 5;
69, 2; 87, 5; 95, 3;
96, 1; 98, 3; 113, 5;
114, 3; 125, 5; 126, 2;
141, 6; 142, 5; 156, 3;
164, 7; 165, 4; 205, 5;
207, 8; 213, 9; 216, 8;
223, 2; 229, 1; 231, 9;
241, 9; 242, 5; 248, 1;
258, 7; 262, 2
Faces 125, 8
Fact 1, 1; 33, 9;
46, 2; 52, 2; 61, 7;
71, 6; 80, 5; 99, 3;
99, 7; 118, 6; 129, 4;
130, 7; 137, 8; 162, 7;
171, 6; 172, 2; 187, 6;
189, 2; 198, 5; 203, 4;
212, 7; 228, 1;
244, 4; 252, 8; 257, 6;
268, 7; 270, 1
Factor 137, 7; 161, 5
Facts 29, 9; 77, 6; 171, 1;
239, 6; 270, 1
Faculty 201, 8
Failure 36, 1; 63, 5;
115, 4; 133, 2; 148, 6;
182, 4; 214, 3
Failures 91, 2; 217, 4
Fair 169, 9; 202, 1
Fair Play 225, 1
Fair-weather 164, 6
Faith 8, 6;
36, 2; 76, 9; 77, 9;

85, 5; 87, 1; 119, 4; 120, 8;
138, 1; 139, 7; 141, 1;
164, 2; 195, 9; 198, 3
Fall 18, 3; 48, 7; 60, 4;
109, 2; 110, 6; 168, 8;
185, 5; 222, 4
Falling 68, 8; 143, 7;
196, 2
Falls 152, 8
Falsehood 77, 7;
97, 6
Fame 23, 1; 77, 8;
176, 3; 180, 5; 183, 2
Family 49, 6; 80, 4;
98, 1; 205, 6; 209, 5; 231, 8;
235, 2; 249, 4; 267, 2
Familiarity 267, 2
Fanaticism 91, 8; 258, 9
Fangs 70, 7
Fantastic 10, 7; 126, 1
Fantasy 87, 2
Farmer 172, 5; 176, 9;
237, 7; 241, 2
Fashion 56, 4
Fast 32, 2; 41, 2;
50, 1; 97, 3; 113, 6;
150, 6; 209, 2; 216, 6;
234, 8; 272, 4
Fat 18, 7; 40, 5;
215, 3; 229, 6
Fate 94, 1; 100, 1
Father 32, 3; 112, 1;
180, 9; 206, 3; 234, 7;
257, 5
Father Time 119, 6
Fathom 87, 2; 213, 2
Fault 4, 5; 44, 8;
69, 1; 100, 1; 122, 1;
160, 4; 182, 2; 220, 1;
251, 6
Faultfinding 132, 8
Faults 122, 1; 124, 1;
125, 5; 127, 9; 130, 1;
136, 5; 199, 8; 211, 5;
228, 2
Favor 12, 5; 22, 2;

Hatch 55, 7; 188, 5;
227, 6
Hate 30, 2; 30, 4; 50, 1;
71, 4; 101, 4; 137, 1;
139, 8; 157, 2; 166, 3;
180, 8; 187, 8; 193, 4;
216, 3; 218, 3; 231, 1;
231, 7; 240, 3; 255, 4
Haters 19, 5
Hating 72, 7
Hatrack 198, 3
Hatred 15, 3; 18, 7;
22, 1; 48, 5; 131, 7
Having 93, 8
Haystack 238, 6
Head 67, 4; 79, 7;
80, 3; 81, 3; 89, 3;
105, 1; 126, 1; 180, 3;
190, 8; 202, 2; 217, 2;
222, 4; 230, 4; 237, 5;
241, 5; 243, 2; 255, 1;
259, 3
Headache 175, 4; 246, 5
Headline 28, 7
Heads 53, 6; 221, 5;
232, 9
Headwaters 145, 9
Headway 6, 5
Health 17, 1
Hearing 131, 4
Heart 9, 7; 10, 1; 17, 7; 18, 2;
20, 7; 22, 3; 24, 6; 36, 6;
42, 2; 50, 4; 52, 8;
56, 7; 61, 1; 62, 2;
64, 3; 66, 2; 90, 3;
91, 1; 92, 3;
92, 8; 94, 7; 96, 5;
97, 2; 101, 1; 104, 4;
107, 1; 109, 8;   110, 1;
111, 4; 117, 5; 119, 3;
121, 3; 122, 2;
122, 4; 138, 1; 139, 4;
142, 3; 143, 9; 148, 5;
150, 2; 158, 7; 164, 3;
172, 3; 183, 6; 185, 3;
190, 3; 190, 5; 192, 6;

193, 3; 193, 7; 203, 7; 212, 3;
216, 9; 242, 6; 266, 5
Heartache 31, 4; 62, 9;
70, 8; 221, 10
Heartaches 195, 7
Hearth 170, 9; 202, 8
Hearts 38, 7; 53, 6;
61, 3; 63, 6; 68, 9;
144, 8; 240, 8
Heat 23, 7; 145, 2
Heaven 22, 8;
77, 2; 96, 5;
121, 2; 150, 4; 179, 4;
195, 1; 243, 4; 267, 7
Heels 76, 1; 78, 4;
89, 4; 136, 3; 216, 5
Height 138, 2
Heights 109, 2
Heir 150, 7
Heiress 52, 2
Heirloom 181, 7
Heirs 141, 5; 159, 7;
169, 9; 178, 3; 271, 2
Hell 22, 8; 46, 1; 68, 5;
77, 2; 174, 7; 195, 1;
207, 6; 221, 5; 248, 7
Hellcat 152, 6
Help 57, 9; 130, 7;
143, 1; 152, 4
Hen 50, 9; 80, 2; 143, 3;
188, 5; 251, 3
Herbs 175, 6
Heredity 102, 7; 188, 8; 235, 7
Hermaphrodite 180, 9
Hesitation 184, 1
Hiding 79, 8; 125, 1;
166, 5; 206, 5; 206, 8
Highway 127, 8; 195, 4
Hills 46, 1; 86, 8
Historians 268, 2
History 107, 5;
163, 4; 174, 1; 197, 7;
226, 10; 239, 8
Hit 38, 8; 44, 3;
129, 6; 146, 2
Hobby 154, 4; 208, 9

Ink 66, 5
In-laws 15, 4
Inmates 246, 6
Innocence 22, 6
Impossibility 11, 8;
24, 4
Insect 237, 7
Insects 163, 5
Insight 67, 6; 155, 1;
190, 4; 213, 3
Insignificance 63, 2;
74, 3; 208, 2; 221, 9;
263, 2
Inspiration 39, 2; 46, 8;
265, 5
Inspirations 192, 1
Instability 135, 1
Installment 80, 6
Instance 148, 9
Instances 219, 2
Instinct 49, 8; 51, 4;
57, 2; 73, 1; 140, 1;
189, 8; 207, 7; 222, 1;
226, 1; 227, 6; 246, 3;
252, 6; 272, 7
Instinctively 225, 2
Instincts 92, 1; 98, 7
Institution 246, 6
Institutions 134, 7; 269, 5
Insults 56, 6
Insurance 117, 6; 166, 3;
196, 5; 214, 5
Insurmountable 92, 8
Integrity 38, 5; 107, 7
Intellect 269, 5
Intellectual 160, 3
Intelligence 46, 2; 71, 6;
88, 1; 100, 5; 122, 8;
124, 3; 138, 2; 161, 5;
218, 7; 231, 8; 267, 6
Intensity 80, 9
Intent 4, 9; 126, 2;
157, 8; 254, 10; 262, 1;
266, 7
Intention 24, 2; 53, 3;
156, 2; 218, 8

Intentions 31, 3; 130, 3
Intents 151, 2
Interest 129, 1; 154, 4;
171, 4; 233, 5
Interior 119, 5
Interpretation 189, 1
Intolerance 64, 4; 145, 5;
180, 8; 231, 1
Intoxicants 10, 3
Intoxicated 71, 5
Intoxication 124, 1
Intuition 233, 7
Invasion 179, 4
Invention 180, 9
Inventory 23, 2; 132, 5
Investment 96, 4; 237, 7
Invitation 56, 4
Involving 173, 6
Iota 131, 6
Iron 62, 6; 82, 6;
140, 6; 188, 4
Irritation 218, 1
Itch 183, 3; 254, 8
Itches 231, 5
Itching 69, 6; 93, 6;
254, 8
Ivy 69, 6; 210, 3

J

Jackass 235, 4;
241, 7
Jail 47, 6; 58, 4;
90, 4; 104, 2; 110, 5;
154, 1; 270, 7
Jam 35, 10
Jar 259, 10
Jaw 56, 8
Jaws 92, 6
Jaws 92, 7; 109, 8
Jealousy 104, 4;
136, 7; 154, 5; 158, 7
Jesting 5, 2
Jewels 66, 8
Jingle 33, 8

146, 2; 146, 8;
193, 3
Laughter 90, 6; 141, 4;
146, 8; 184, 3
Law 45, 4; 72, 9; 74, 3;
106, 4; 154, 1; 168, 5;
168, 8; 178, 4;
183, 1; 200, 3; 226, 10;
228, 1; 236, 5; 253, 9;
269, 7
Lawn 121, 4; 261, 1
Laws 81, 6; 83, 7; 91, 3;
134, 7; 269, 1
Lawyers 154, 3
Lead 10, 5; 28, 6;
108, 6; 109, 8; 172, 6;
270, 7
Leader 137, 8
Learned 63, 3; 82, 2;
88, 6; 149, 4; 161, 1;
210, 5
Leash 270, 7
Leaves 33, 2; 68, 8;
111, 5; 140, 9; 153, 6;
170, 8
Ledger 154, 7; 171, 8
Leech 143, 9
Leg 65, 6; 145, 6
Legacy 213, 1
Legal 241, 8
Legalize 196, 4
Legs 97, 6
Leisure 219, 9
Land 65, 4
Lenient 26, 7
Lethargy 247, 1
Letter 41, 5
Level 185, 10
Level headed235, 10
Levers 226, 1
Liability 35, 2; 75, 2
Liable 57, 6; 151, 4;
222, 4
Liar 56, 1; 135, 6; 248, 1
Liberal 68, 7
Liberalism 241, 4

Liberty 96, 9
Lice 241, 5
License 36, 8; 84, 1;
184, 9; 223, 4
Lid 173, 3
Lie 34, 9; 46, 3;
120, 8; 147, 8; 152, 5;
157, 6; 193, 3; 248, 1;
265, 4
Lies 56, 1; 95, 7;
114, 7; 254, 2
Life 1, 4; 3, 1; 3, 4; 6, 2;
8, 5; 9, 6; 16, 5;
18, 3; 22, 2; 22, 3;
25, 4; 29, 5; 29, 8;
31, 5; 32, 2; 37, 5;
41, 8; 41, 9; 43, 4;
52, 5; 52, 6; 52, 7;
53, 2; 60, 4; 60, 7;
63, 5; 64, 8; 66, 7;
68, 1; 68, 8; 72, 7;
73, 6; 74, 2;
75, 1; 77, 1; 80, 8;
86, 7; 88, 3; 88, 4;
89, 1; 92, 1; 92, 3;
92, 7; 94, 6; 94, 8;
95, 9; 96, 4; 96, 7;
97, 5; 102, 8; 103, 4;
103, 5; 109, 7; 110, 6;
112, 5; 113, 6; 114, 5;
114, 8; 116, 8; 116, 10;
117, 6; 118, 7; 119, 5;
119, 8; 123, 4; 126, 5;
127, 1; 129, 2; 130, 6; 131, 7;
132, 7; 134, 3; 134, 5;
135, 9; 136, 3; 136, 4;
138, 6; 139, 1; 139, 6;
140, 1; 142, 5; 142, 6;
143, 6; 144, 8; 148, 2;
153, 1; 157, 4; 159, 7;
160, 2; 161, 5; 162, 7;
162, 8; 164, 5; 164, 8;
166, 1; 166, 8; 168, 5;
171, 7; 171, 8; 172, 6;
174, 6; 175, 1; 177, 9; 178, 1;
180, 1; 186, 1; 187, 6;

Meandering 204, 6
Measure 224, 2; 270, 6
Meat 20, 4; **32, 5**
Medal 43, 3
Medicine 168, 8
Mediocrity 252, 7
Melody 122, 5; 219, 7
Memories 13, 3; **38, 7;**
40, 3; 42, 9; 115, 3
Memory 15, 2; 31, 4; 39, 2;
75, 1; 92, 2; 100, 6;
172, 1; 205, 4
Men 22, 7; 23, 1; 30, 8;
32, 6; 33, 9; 43, 4; 51, 1;
52, 2; 54, 5; 55, 2;
56, 6; 73, 7; 78, 6;
81, 4; 81, 6; 82, 4;
83, 8; 85, 6; 104, 6;
110, 4; 110, 7; 110, 8;
113, 8; 129, 9; 141, 5;
146, 7; 173, 8; 181, 4;
191, 8; 196, 1; 197, 1;
200, 4; 205, 9; 212, 7;
222, 2; 225, 2; 228, 3;
229, 1; 233, 6; 236, 2;
238, 3; 244, 3; 245, 4;
266, 6; 271, 4; 272, 5
Menagerie 82, 7
Mend 185, 5
Mental 130, 8; 246, 6
Mentality 107, 6
Merchant 181, 1
Mercy 197, 1
Merge 90, 1
Merry-go-round 160, 7
Mess 149, 6
Metamorphic 267, 1
Meteorites 132, 2
Method 161, 5
Microscope 33, 3; 202, 7
Midway 87, 6
Might 28, 2; **48, 3;**
111, 6; 137, 6; 138, 1;
143, 3; 144, 3; 154, 7;
161, 6; 164, 9; 179, 4;
196, 7

Mile 52, 6; 191, 5
Milepost 41, 9
Miles 127, 8; 215, 4
Milk 18, 7; 262, 5;
268, 6
Mill 182, 8; 208, 5
Million 33, 7; 52, 6;
79, 3; 84, 9; 157, 1;
196, 9; 263, 4
Millionaire 48, 3
Millionaires 83, 6
Millions 53, 3; 121, 2;
128, 2; 142, 6
Millstone 64, 1; 201, 2;
240, 2
Mind 10, 1; 10, 8; 13, 6;
14, 3; 14, 6; 15, 6;
20, 8; 21, 8; 30, 3; 34, 2;
35, 10; 36, 1; 39, 8;
44, 4; 46, 6; 50, 4;
53, 8; 56, 7; 57, 7;
62, 5; 64, 3; 72, 4;
73, 8; 81, 1; 83, 1;
97, 2; 103, 8; 105, 4;
107, 4; 116, 2; 118, 5;
122, 3; 124, 4; 129, 10;
136, 6; 138, 1; 147, 2;
147, 3; 149, 2; 152, 4;
153, 8; 156, 4; 157, 1; 157, 3;
158, 6; 158, 7; 159, 2;
159, 9; 166, 7; 168, 8;
174, 4; 176, 7; 177, 5;
181, 5; 182, 2; 183, 5;
184, 8; 185, 8;
190, 3; 192, 1; 194, 3;
195, 7; 197, 6; 201, 1;
203, 7; 204, 4; 206, 2;
209, 7; 212, 1; 213, 2;
213, 9; 214, 3; 216, 7;
218, 3; 221, 6; 223, 2;
224, 1; 224, 2; 226, 5;
226, 9; 231, 9; 240, 1;
242, 7; 258, 9;
261, 1; 262, 4; 265, 4;
268, 7; 271, 7; 272, 6
Minds 68, 9; 144, 8;

Newness 236, 8
Newspapers 156, 3
Nibble 81, 1
Nickel 187, 4
Nickels 229, 3
Night 57, 3; 90, 1; 114, 6;
139, 2; 174, 3; 231, 9
Nipple 244, 3
Nobility 214, 4
Noble 178, 8
Noise 76, 6; 235, 5
Noonday 128, 1
Noose 49, 9; 91, 2
Nose 10, 5; 17, 2;
28, 6; 52, 5; 64, 4;
186, 7; 210, 1; 213, 7;
215, 5
Note 42, 1; 57, 6;
74, 8; 95, 10; 191, 1;
244, 1
Nothingness 139, 1
Notice 37, 1; 72, 2;
81, 8; 84, 3; 100, 3;
110, 8; 112, 8; 113, 9;
123, 7; 155, 5; 198, 1;
234, 8
Nourishment 94, 9
Novel 109, 7; 263, 5
Nude 34, 6; 118, 2
Nugget 102, 3
Nuisance 77, 5
Number 95, 2; 124, 4
Numbers 172, 7
Numerals 207, 9
Nutshell 31, 5

O

Oak 47, 4
Obedience 130, 8
Obedient 168, 5
Obituary 11, 6
Object 42, 8; 207, 2
Obligation 134, 3; 229, 9;
241, 8; 258, 8

Obnoxious 188, 9
Observation 197, 7;
236, 8; 254, 9
Obstruction 272, 4
Occasion 113, 1; 210, 4
Occasions 155, 4
Ocean 109, 4; 195, 8;
197, 1
Oceans 62, 9
Octopus 93, 1; 122, 7;
136, 1
Odds 22, 2; 84, 9
Odor 68, 2; 145, 6
Offer 61, 1; 177, 2
Offspring 129, 8;
201, 5; 234, 1
Oil 9, 4; 49, 5;
99, 5; 113, 1; 148, 4
Old Age 145, 7; 152, 10
Old Man Responsibility
206, 5
Oldsters 184, 3
Olive 146, 9; 259, 6
Ooze 208, 8
Opinion 47, 2; 209, 8;
248, 8; 270, 4
Opponent 35, 10; 75, 3;
201, 1; 223, 5
Opponents 220, 3
Opportunist 243, 2
Opportunities 28, 7
Opportunity 9, 5; 17, 2;
30,1; 41, 3; 125, 1; 144, 7;
162, 6; 164, 1; 166, 2;
184, 1; 186, 4; 203, 4;
214, 2; 259, 4
Opposition 257, 4
Optimism 145, 1; 145, 4
Optimist 26, 1; 31, 1;
65, 6; 125, 7; 148, 5; 202, 7
Orchard 136, 6
Orchestra 84, 7
Orchid 100, 5; 140, 3
Orchids 29, 6; 140, 3
Ordeal 91, 4
Order 97, 1; 106, 4;

Pinhead 243, 2
Pinheads 221, 5
Pinnacle 140, 8
Pip squeak 235, 3
Pitchfork 148, 7
Pity 78, 6; 194, 5
Place 35, 2; 44, 6;
79, 8; 89, 4; 114, 1;
139, 4; 143, 1; 156, 5;
164, 1; 177, 7; 227, 8;
228, 1; 232, 7; 242, 8;
247, 8; 259, 5; 267, 6;
272, 1
Places 58, 6; 95, 6;
108, 3; 129, 4; 141, 6;
147, 1; 147, 6; 200, 9
Plague 91, 8
Plain 54, 5
Plan 79, 9; 104, 1;
114, 4; 158, 4
Plane 139, 1
Planet 102, 8
Planned 46, 2
Plans 79, 5
Plant 95, 5; 140, 3;
166, 2; 171, 5; 234, 5;
237, 7
Plants 40, 5; 40, 8;
74, 1
Plate 112, 8
Platter 61, 1
Play 39, 4; 52, 4;
66, 8; 73, 2; 111, 2;
127, 2; 183, 6; 193, 7;
202, 1; 225, 1
Player 103, 4; 104, 8;
225, 1
Playmate 85, 1
Plays 172, 1; 186, 1;
205, 7
Pleasure 32, 2; 58, 5;
130, 4; 147, 7; 189, 4;
245, 7
Plenty 125, 2
Plight 97, 3
Plow 91, 1

Pocket 151, 5; 178, 5;
190, 2
Pockets 88, 2; 107, 1
Pod 139, 8
Pods 189, 7
Poem 189, 7
Poetry 52, 5
Poets 16, 5
Point 69, 9; 150, 3;
198, 8; 257, 3
Points 155, 2
Poison 34, 2; 66, 5;
69, 6; 100, 4; 143, 2;
210, 3
Poisonous 95, 6
Poisons 104, 4
Poker 116, 5; 228, 4
Polish 236, 8
Politeness 254, 6
Politics 20, 2; 39, 4;
146, 5; 204, 6
Politician 3, 6; 106, 1
Politicians 39, 4
Poor 77, 8
Poorhouse 90, 8
Popularity 108, 4; 134, 9
Populated 95, 1
Population 42, 4
Position 86, 5
Positions 183, 7
Positive 8, 5; 145, 1
Possess 77, 4
Possession 24, 1;
72, 9; 156, 4; 173, 2
Possessions 132, 5
Posterity 78, 2; 163, 7
Pot 216, 6
Potato 47, 5
Potential 74, 9; 137, 8
Potentiality 146, 1
Potter's Field 42, 5
Poverty 53, 1; 57, 5; 99, 5;
106, 7; 153, 4; 172, 2;
178, 6; 188, 6; 221, 4
Powder 93, 6
Power 140, 8; 144, 6;

Protein 242, 8
Protest 40, 4
Protestations 34, 2
Provider 82, 4
Proximity 204, 1
Prune 136, 6
Public 20, 2; 79, 3;
116, 2; 171, 4;
255, 6
Publicity 180, 5
Pudle 73, 5; 80, 8;
217, 3
Puffs 60, 8
Pull 120, 5; 159, 9;
203, 2; 259, 7
Pulse 22, 3
Pulverizing 182, 8;
208, 5
Punchboard 69, 5
Punishment 4, 6; 28, 4;
78, 1; 120, 1; 163, 1;
193, 10
Pupa 267, 1
Purity 101, 5; 159, 6;
188, 1
Purpose 19, 1; 44, 9;
55, 9; 60, 6; 165, 2;
249, 1; 266, 7
Purposes 151, 2
Purse 94, 7; 262, 1
Puzzle 9, 9

Q

Qualifications 23, 2
Qualities 124, 1; 227, 5;
238, 2
Quandary 197, 4
Quantity 66, 1; 262, 5
Quarrel 29, 4; 97, 1;
250, 8
Quarrels 141, 9
Quartz 143, 6
Queen 38, 3

Quicksand 196, 2
Quota 96, 7; 242, 8

R

Race 51, 8; 55, 6;
75, 3; 84, 4; 108, 5;
110, 6; 114, 5; 225, 7;
228, 6
Races 88, 7; 232, 3
Radiance 54, 3; 134, 9;
180, 8; 181, 2
Radio 134, 8
Radish 225, 4
Raft 137, 7
Rafters 67, 4
Rage 183, 7
Rain 37, 2; 37, 8;
112, 3; 121, 3; 124, 5
Rainbow 125, 4; 138, 6
Rapture 14, 5; 22, 3
Ratio 108, 4
Rats 164, 6
Rattle 98, 7
Razor 138, 5
Reaching 192, 1
Realistic 260, 9
Reality 23, 5; 34, 6;
75, 3; 139, 5; 154, 2;
190, 4; 223, 2; 258, 9
Realization 138, 3;
243, 8
Reaper 137, 3
Reason 3, 5; 25, 6;
29, 3; 32, 8; 49, 8;
51, 4; 60, 4; 113, 9;
117, 8; 136, 7; 154, 2;
154, 5; 189, 8; 196, 3;
214, 3; 219, 1; 224, 7;
257, 4; 262, 8; 266, 6
Reasoning 27, 4; 94, 2;
190, 8; 201, 8; 209, 4;
226, 1; 235, 9
Reasons 29, 3; 85, 6;
176, 1; 177, 7; 189, 1;

Skull 198, 1; 264, 2
Skunk 86, 8; 258, 8
Skunks 240, 4
Sky 46, 4; 63, 2;
112, 3; 115, 6; 125, 4;
161, 2; 210, 4
Slander 16, 4
Slave 2, 3; 38, 3;
57, 8; 103, 7; 237, 6
Slavery 124, 3
Slaves 99, 1; 237, 6
Slaving 201, 6
Sledge-hammer 63, 5
Sleep 16, 1; 40, 7;
41, 8; 93, 4; 117, 4;
142, 6; 165, 2; 186, 1;
198, 8; 262, 4
Sling 96, 3
Sly 41, 1; 159, 1
Smallness 73, 8
Smallpox 231, 1
Smell 30, 2; 193, 8;
215, 5; 207, 3; 218, 1
Smile 96, 1; 106, 1;
119, 3; 141, 6; 164, 7;
224, 7; 247, 6; 266, 7;
269, 3
Smiling 125, 8
Smithy 140, 6
Smoke 37, 8; 101, 2;
170, 9
Smother 87, 1
Smouldering 23, 7; 95, 8
Snap 124, 9; 199, 1
Snarling 43, 5; 82, 7
Snatch 150, 6
Snatching 160, 7; 186, 4
Sneaking 125, 1
Sniff 145, 6
Snob 176, 4
Snow 190, 3
Snowfall 32, 4
Snub 114, 8
Soap 65, 3
Sobbing 123, 3
Social 163, 6

Society 86, 5; 103, 5
Sockets 84, 1
Soil 101, 4
Sole 216, 9
Soles 258, 5
Solitude 40, 3
Solution 164, 4
Somebody 119, 2
Someday 66, 3
Something 39, 5; 50, 1;
67, 5; 83, 2; 87, 4;
91, 3; 101, 1; 116, 6;
119, 2; 147, 2; 148, 4;
157, 4; 234, 6
Son 76, 2; 112, 1;
161, 9; 163, 1; 257, 5
Song 92, 3; 115, 1;
150, 2
Sore 188, 7
Sorrow 37, 6; 42, 9;
46, 5; 95, 10
Soul 30, 4; 31, 2; 33, 8;
35, 8; 36, 6; 42, 1;
54, 7; 142, 7; 153, 6;
187, 7; 190, 5
Souls 100, 6; 161, 7
Sound 27, 5; 90, 2
Sounds 199, 8
Space 52, 6; 123, 1;
131, 4; 215, 8
Spadework 270, 5
Span 119, 5
Spank 1, 1
Spark 66, 5; 112, 5;
119, 5; 137, 1;
154, 6; 162, 7; 170, 2;
198, 4; 202, 8; 215, 6
Sparklers 82, 4
Sparks 57, 9; 169, 4
Sparrow 185, 4
Specialization 225, 6
Species 82, 7; 103, 1; 218, 9
Specimen 78, 2
Speck 134, 3
Speech 255, 8
Speed 96, 2; 145, 10;

253, 4
Speeds 176, 9
Spell 144, 6
Spendthrift 5, 8
Sphere 231, 4
Spice 53, 2; 66, 7;
148, 2
Spice of life 11, 8
Spinner 51, 9
Spinster 99, 2
Spirit 44, 9; 55, 9;
78, 7; 93, 2; 250, 7
Spiritual 138, 1
Spite 75, 3
Splatter 96, 3
Spoil 141, 3
Sponge 226, 5
Sponges 195, 8
Spoons 54, 2
Sport 123, 6
Spot 243, 5
Spots 39, 1; 114, 4;
200, 1
Spring 25, 4; 102, 7; 107, 7;
201, 1
Sprout 25, 3; 47, 4;
68, 6; 116, 6; 122, 8;
139, 8; 149, 7; 165, 4;
181, 6
Spur 55, 6; 189, 6
Squabble 272, 6
Squall 107, 7; 115, 8
Squalls 151, 1
Squander 12, 8; 169, 9
Squeeze 252, 1
Stability 132, 4
Stack 83, 3
Stage 81, 4;
179, 3; 201, 8
Stains 30, 4
Stake 103, 4
Stalls 80, 6
Stamina 23, 1; 63, 5
Stand 50, 9; 165, 6;
179, 5; 196, 8; 217, 2;
270, 7

Standards 106, 4; 110, 7
Stands 152, 8
Star 157, 1; 269, 7
Starlit 63, 2
Stars 35, 5; 62, 4;
121, 2; 194, 5
Starving 50, 5; 58, 3;
83, 4; 92, 2
State 156, 3; 159, 2;
267, 1
Statesman 26, 6; 76, 3; 111, 3
Statistics 213, 8
Status 163, 6; 270, 1
Stay-at-homes 103, 1
Steal 19, 3; 62, 1;
98, 8; 100, 7; 211, 9;
212, 8; 216, 6
Stealing 40, 6; 79, 4;
217, 8
Steam 187, 5
Steel 212, 6
Stench 133, 3
Step 195, 2; 243, 7
Steppingstones 35, 6;
44, 5
Stick 233, 9; 264, 7
Stigma 147, 2
Stillness 90, 1
Stilts 162, 2
Stimulation 49, 2; 81, 4
Sting 124, 9
Stinger 255, 1
Stingers 73, 7
Stink 194, 1; 240, 4;
252, 2
Stinkeroo 98, 1
Stinkers 152, 7
Stinkweed 140, 3
Stinkweeds 10, 6;
37, 3
Stock 175, 2
Stomach 21, 4; 36, 6;
44, 9; 70, 4; 72, 1;
153, 4; 177, 1; 236, 3
Stomachs 94, 9
Stone 1, 4; 92, 8; 164, 8;

Twitch 98, 2
Tycoon 62, 8
Type 214, 4
Types 106, 8
Tyrant 132, 2; 250, 4
Tyrants 62, 6; 267, 4
Tyranny 154, 2; 231, 4

U

Ulcers 110, 8; 236, 3; 263, 4
Ulterior 128, 5; 148, 7
Ultimate 34, 2; 54, 6; 88, 4; 148, 2; 195, 6
Uncertainty 1, 2; 232, 2
Uncle 110, 3; 111, 2
Uncle Sam 169, 9
Unconsciousness 211, 8
Underdog 175, 3
Underpinnings 152, 8
Understand 93, 4
Understanding 215, 8
Undertaking 182, 4; 239, 3
Union 22, 3; 148, 2; 172, 7
Unions 268, 2
United States 1, 1
United World 128, 2
Unity 172, 7; 184, 6
Universe 25, 5; 83, 7; 94, 1
Untruth 135, 6
Uppercut 108, 7
Upset 107, 6; 112, 2
Usefulness 32, 1

V

Vacuum 90, 2

Value 35, 4; 50, 10; 117, 3; 187, 4; 247, 3
Values 71, 3; 124, 6
Vanity 134, 2; 153, 8; 157, 6
Variation 135, 6
Varieties 195, 8
Variety 51, 2; 139, 8; 195, 8
Vat 48, 7
Vegetable 152, 7
Veil 119, 3
Veins 143, 9
Velocity 44, 7
Veneer 91, 5
Venom 104, 4
Venture 120, 5
Verbiage 191, 5
Vice 45, 4; 171, 4; 243, 3
Victim 64, 4; 136, 1
Victims 152, 3; 184, 4; 259, 5
Victory 109, 6; 209, 3
View 72, 9; 193, 6; 198, 8; 255, 6; 263, 6
Vigilance 262, 1
Vigor 165, 4; 176, 3
Violins 183, 6
Virtue 5, 4
Vision 79, 3; 161, 8
Visual 60, 2
Vitamins 98, 6
Vitriolic 188, 7
Voice 76, 3; 107, 2; 154, 5; 158, 2; 182, 3; 209, 6; 269, 4
Voices 17, 3; 78, 5; 142, 6
Void 102, 1; 135, 7; 140, 1; 142, 2
Voltage 109, 5
Vote 267, 4
Vulgarity 7, 7
Vultures 265, 6

PN 6281 .H84 1961

Hurwitt, Samuel Jacob

A treasury of epigrams

WITHDRAWN

SEO Library Center
State Library of Ohio

40780 Marietta Road, Caldwell, OH 43724

DEMCO